The Five Approaches to Acting Series

TELLING A STORY

WRITTEN BY DAVID KAPLAN

Hansen Publishing Group, LLC
East Brunswick, New Jersey
www.hansenpublishing.com

The Five Approaches to Acting Series: Telling a Story
Copyright © 2007 David Kaplan

International Standard Book Number: 978-1-60182-185-0

H P G **Hansen Publishing Group, LLC**
302 Ryders Lane
East Brunswick, New Jersey
732-220-1211
www.hansenpublishing.com

CREDITS

To Edwin W. Schloss,

Prince of friends, open-hearted, open-eyed.

CONTENTS

SCRIPT ANALYSIS COMPARATIVE REFERENCE CHART

	TASK/ACTION ANALYSIS	EPISODIC ANALYSIS	BUILDING IMAGES ANALYSIS	WORLD OF THE PLAY ANALYSIS	NARRATIVE ANALYSIS
BASIC UNIT	Task	Episode	Image	Social context; behavior and form	Event Point of view
ILLUSION OF CHARACTER	Web of relationships	Playing the opposition	String of masks	Distinctions within the context of the world	Intersection of point of view and events
DRAMATIC ACTION	Action meeting an obstacle	Transaction or *gest*	Moment when mask changes	Breach in the rules of the world	Shifting the point of view
KEY QUESTION	What do I need to do?	What do I do? What is my role?	What is this like? What does this make me think of?	What are the values of the world?	What am I describing? What is my point of view?
UNIFYING IMAGE	Oil painting	Poster	Collage	Frame	Film camera angles
RELATIVE THEORY	Freud Psychoanalysis	Alfred Adler Transactional analysis Marxism	Carl Jung Personae	Ruth Benedict Cultural anthropology	Derrida Literary decon-structionism
SUITABLE PLAYWRIGHTS	Chekhov Ibsen Strindberg	Shakespeare Brecht Ionesco	Strindberg Lorca Genet Williams	Molière Wilde O'Neill Beckett	Shakespeare the Greeks Williams Shepard
AUDIENCE	Compassionate	Judgmental	Passionate	Transported	Participatory

PART V

TELLING A STORY

Reading List
Iphigenia in Aulis by Euripides
Buried Child by Sam Shepard
Stories from other plays cited as examples are included in the text

Viewing List
Long Day's Journey into Night directed by Sidney Lumet

René Magritte, detail from *The Glass House*

CHAPTER 1

STORYTELLING

In the Theater of the Audience's Mind

Telling stories dates back to the caves. Telling stories in plays probably dates back to the Greeks, and has persisted ever since. When that prototype Method actor Polus (Chapter 8) tottered out onstage in 511 BCE carrying his dead son's ashes in order to mourn Orestes, the audience was prepared to sob along with him because another character in the play had previously told the story of how Orestes died in a chariot race. When Helene Weigel first caught Brecht's eye, she was delivering the Servant's speech in *Oedipus the King* that describes the death of Jocasta, the hero's wife and mother. When the fifteen-year-old Sarah Bernhardt auditioned for the Paris Conservatory, she forgot to bring a copy of the scene she had prepared. Since no one could feed her cues, she told a story instead, and her rendition of a children's fable about two pigeons was so moving that her auditioners' initial giggles gave way to open tears (85).

Classic, romantic, or modern—storytelling persists in theatrical tradition because in all times and all places it renews its contributions to the performance of a play. Stories told as performances depict dramatic action that the stage could not otherwise depict: ungodly horror, the glory of the gods, a battle at sea. Stories told in the course of a play refine the actor's expression of thought and memory. Stories told onstage expand the audience's vision to include what individual characters cannot see, or understand, or want known—even about themselves. Be it soliloquy or gossip, revelation or panorama or report, the action of a play doesn't stop or even pause when a character onstage tells a story; the action proceeds, but on a different plane.

Yet, storytelling braided into the action of a play is not always subject to the same rules as impersonation. An actor telling a story onstage can use a technique specific to storytelling, a technique different from any he might employ while acting out a role in a scene. Since Shakespeare's soliloquies offer performers and audiences such a wide range of action, vision, and personal investigation, they will be considered separately, in Chapter 13.

Storytelling as Illusion

Onstage—as opposed to in a living room or a courtroom—storytelling is an illusion. You are not really remembering what happened; you are not really reporting what can be seen offstage. What's happening offstage? The actors are flirting with each other in the wings, or playing cards, or staring into their dressing room mirrors, or sipping from flasks. Whether reminiscing, reporting, or delivering a message, an actor tells a story onstage so the audience can picture what's being described.

That bears repeating (so that you can repeat it too): *An actor is telling a story so the audience can picture what the story describes.*

The power to place an image in other people's minds, and to make that image vivid enough to arouse listeners to emotions of their own, is rightly called *casting a spell—spell* being related to the German word *spiel*, for "story." Radio plays, bedtime stories, ghost stories, erotic stories—any of these are familiar examples of how a storyteller can make a listener turn the mind into an amphitheater, a boudoir, or any place the action described is occurring. Casting a spell is much more wonderful than deep-felt reminiscence; the whole value of a story, on the stage and in life, is that a story transcends the personal and becomes a form of shared vision, wider than an individual's. This magic is repeated onstage whenever a story is told. Yes, it helps to have a vision of what you are describing, but even performers who believe in their visions as spiritual revelations have to share their insight with the congregation.

The Advantages of Storytelling: From Aeschylus to Sam Shepard

Past and present, and in all cultures, playwrights have returned to storytelling in the course of a play because telling a story offers a heightened dimension with which to express dramatic action. In the West, telling stories has been part of theater from its historical origins. Let's review a few texts from the Western repertory that we can use later as examples.

A vision that exceeds the possibilities of life

The Persians (86) was written by the Greek playwright Aeschylus in 472 BCE. It describes events that occurred eight years before the play was written: the defeat of the vast Persian navy by the small ships assembled from the Greek city-states. There is no battle shown onstage; it is described. The scene takes place at the court of Persia. A chorus of old men and the Queen wait to hear news from the front. A Messenger arrives. He describes a rout:

> MESSENGER At first by its huge impetus
> Our fleet withstood them. But soon, in that narrow space,
> Our ships were jammed in hundreds; none could help another.
> They rammed each other with their prows of bronze; and some
> Were stripped of every oar. Meanwhile the enemy
> Came round us in a ring and charged. Our vessels heeled
> Over; the sea was hidden, carpeted with wrecks
> And dead men; all the shores and reefs were full of dead.

Then every ship we had broke rank and rowed for life.
The Greeks seized fragments or wrecks and broken oars
And hacked and stabbed at our men swimming in the sea
As fishermen kill their catch inside a net.

The Persians

If you begin to prepare your performance of this text by identifying *tasks*, as described in Chapter 1, you will have begun your own losing battle. What is the Messenger's task in telling this story of the disastrous Persian defeat to the Persian Queen? He doesn't have any other than *to tell the story*, and, through his efforts, bring the naval battle onto the stage.

To do the job, it helps to have the episode told, not shown; the Messenger's report can depict what no single person could possibly have seen. Hacked or hacker, each participant in the battle would have been caught up in the immediate experience. Not even if you climbed a mast could you have seen the vast Persian fleet run aground. Told as a story, onstage, the historic Battle of Salamis gains a focus it never had in life.

The clarity of distance—emotional and physical

The physical distance needed to comprehend a panorama has a parallel in the psychological distance needed to comprehend outsized emotions. *Oedipus the King* (87), written by Sophocles around 430 BCE, reaches its climax when the queen, Jocasta, hangs herself and Oedipus, her son, tears out his own eyes. These events are described by a Servant of the Queen's, a role played so effectively by Helene Weigel that Bertolt Brecht wrote about her performance for years after.

SERVANT What happened after that I cannot tell,
   Nor say how the end fell, for with a shriek
   Oedipus burst on us; all eyes were fixed
   On Oedipus, as up and down he stalked,
   Nor could we mark her agony to the end.
   For striding back and forth "A sword!" he cried,
   "Where is my wife, no wife, the teeming womb
   That bore a double harvest, me and mine?"
   And in his frenzy some divine power
   (No man nor woman, none of us who watched him)
   Guided his footsteps; with a terrible shriek,
   As though someone beckoned, he crashed against
   The folding doors, and from the hinges forced
   The wrenched bolts and hurled himself within.
   Then we saw the woman hanging there,
   A running noose was twisted round her neck.
   But when *he* saw her, with a maddened roar

TELLING A STORY

> He untied the cord; and when her wretched corpse
> Lay stretched on earth . . . what followed was horror.

Oedipus the King

If you begin preparation for this speech using the approach of playing an *episode* described in Chapter 5, the question of what is happening onstage can only have one answer: the episode is THE SERVANT TELLS A STORY. What the audience watches onstage is how the speaker is transformed by telling her story. Brecht described how Weigel went from stern pronouncement to begrudging respect to conventional grief to submission. The transaction of the episode is between the speaker and the audience. Brecht puts the transaction as *hear me out / and now you may weep.*

On the simplest level, any story that is an episode has as its transaction: *if the audience pays attention to the speaker / they will hear the story and follow the action of the play.* This is particularly true for the climax of *Oedipus the King*, which would be much more difficult for the audience to understand if they, and not the Servant, witnessed the sights of a suicide by hanging and a man gouging out his own eyes. For most, if not all the spectators, disgust would overwhelm most other responses.

In Greek tragedy, horrors are very often described rather than shown. Potentially vivid theatrical events—the moments you think would attract a playwright to source material in the first place—are usually left offstage. An irreligious king is torn apart by a mob of zealots, a mother kills her children, a wife kills her husband: in Greek tragedies, all these are described after the fact, the better for the action to proceed in the theater of the spectators' minds.

Greek playwrights also used stories to bring the glory of the gods onto the stage. In another play by Sophocles, *Oedipus at Colonus* (88), written forty years after *Oedipus the King*, the hero is assumed by Heaven. How? Again a Messenger speaks:

> MESSENGER The man was gone, he vanished from our eyes;
> We saw only our king whose upraised hand
> Shaded his eyes as from some awful sight,
> That no man might endure to look upon.
> A moment later, and we saw him bend
> In prayer to Earth and prayer to Heaven at once.
> But by what doom the stranger met his end
> No man except Theseus knows.
> For there fell
> No fiery bolt that split him in that hour,
> Nor whirlwind from the sea, but he was taken.
> It was a messenger from heaven, or else
> Some gentle, painless cleaving of earth's base;
> For without wailing or disease or pain
> He passed away—an end most marvelous.

Oedipus at Colonus

Actors telling stories in ancient tragedy can penetrate the depths of horror or ascend to the heavens—all with the playwright's words.

Closer than in life, and behind the façade

In classic ancient comedies, storytelling took on a form it would anywhere, be it Greece or Rome or Albuquerque: *gossip* about the neighbors. As gossip, an actor can tell an audience what is really going on behind the façades of respectable homes.

Prologues set the scene for the audience, explain the background of the plot, and reveal the secret lives and lies of the characters. Despite their name, these Prologues could happen even after the play had started, the better to puncture pretense. *The Braggart Soldier* (*Miles Gloriosus*), written in 205 BCE by the Roman playwright Plautus (89), begins with a dialogue between an obsequious underling and a vainglorious soldier. The flunky can't help but praise his commander's valor, good looks, and success with women. After the soldier and his yes-man exit, out comes a slave, Palaestrio, who explains to the audience just whom and what they've been watching.

> PALAESTRIO This is the city of Ephesus. That soldier who just left for the forum is my master, a stinking shameless blowhard, full of lies and lechery. He says all the women chase after him—actually, wherever he goes, the ladies crack up at the sight of him. You noticed most of the hookers around here have twisted mouths. That's so they don't laugh in his face.
>
> *The Braggart Soldier*

The gossip, often from a slave or a woman, sets out the comic confusion of conventional roles in Roman society: the mighty soldier is a jerk, the respected old senator is randy, his submissive wife is a shrew, his heir a fool, his daughter a ninny, and his slave insubordinate (and usually freer than any citizen). The listening audience for the original productions of these plays shared a world in which slaves and women were excluded from official power; onstage gossip was a way for women and slaves to exercise the force of their own power, by sharing their knowledge of the ruling class in all its hypocrisy.

The collaboration of the audience

In Europe, the dramatic tradition of telling stories ran from the Greek theater to the Roman to the theater of the Middle Ages, which adapted its stories from the Bible and its form of direct address from sermons. Medieval performances were often staged for a faithful illiterate. The story of the scene—and its moral significance—were often repeated to the audience before, during, and after performances.

During the European Renaissance that followed the Age of Faith, attention focused on individuals, rather than categories or moral allegories. There was renewed curiosity, even delight, in the world's variety. Zoos and botanical gardens were established, and portraits were painted to emphasize character and idiosyncrasy, rather than classical beauty or social rank. There was an interest in the drama of individual experience on stages as well, often expressed as stories. There was also a curiosity in the marvels of the past or faraway places, and this, too, could be satisfied on stage with stories that brought the fabulous (a word derived from the Latin *fabula*, or "story") to view. Shakespeare described Cleopatra's barge. Marlowe described the inaccessible Central Asian city of Samarkand. The prolific Spanish playwright Calderón de la Barca described the exotic wilderness of Poland (seen from Spain, Poland seems exotic).

The limited resources of small stages without scenery presented special challenges for playwrights who hoped to present the wonders of history. The events to be dramatized could span decades and, like the naval battle at Salamis, involve a cast of thousands. For Shakespeare, this resulted in a story *about* storytelling, which was probably first delivered by the playwright himself to an audience standing around him, like spectators at a fight:

> CHORUS . . . can this cockpit hold
> The vasty fields of France? Or may we cram
> Within this wooden O the very casques
> That did affright the air at Agincourt?
> O, pardon! Since a crooked figure may
> Attest in little place a million;
> And let us, ciphers to this great company,
> On your imaginary forces work.
> Suppose with the girdle of these walls
> Are now confin'd two mighty monarchies,
> Whose high upreared and abutting fronts
> The perilous narrow ocean parts asunder:
> Piece out our imperfections with your thoughts;
> Into a thousand parts divide one man,
> And make imaginary puissance;
> Think, when we talk of horses. That you see them
> Printing their proud hoofs i' th' receiving earth;
> For 'tis your thoughts that now must deck our kings . . .
>
> *Henry V, Prologue*

This is a basic principle of storytelling on stage: the conversion of words to dramatic action is a *collaboration* between the performer and the audience. The listeners must participate in order for the story to unfold. The performer must present the story in such a way that the listeners can participate.

If we were to approach the Prologue from *Henry V* by building *images*—the technique described in Chapters 7 and 8—the images described in the speech would be more important than any images the speaker might have of himself as the Chorus. In fact, the Chorus says as much. He asks the audience to forget where they are and who is speaking in order to picture in their minds the ocean, the heroes, and the brave horses. The images are the images of the story, and they are evoked in the act of collaboration between speaker and listener. Without the listener, they have no effect.

The images of the story are also ineffectual without the speaker—as voice-over. When Laurence Olivier filmed his 1945 *Henry V*, his biggest problem in the adaptation was how to treat these Chorus speeches. When horses, soldiers, and oceans could be filmed, wouldn't that erase the need for descriptions? Olivier's solution was to start his film with an actor onstage, in a replica of Shakespeare's Globe Theater. This device illustrated perfectly that Shakespeare had written a speech with the power to transport the attention of an audience from reality to vision—a power not unlike a camera's power to command a movie audience's focus and attention. The actor telling a story is presenting—like a camera—close-ups, long shots, or panoramas.

The inner life revealed

Actors speaking Shakespeare's soliloquies can do something a camera cannot: pierce to view the inner life of a role. These stories report the *private thoughts* of a character, which contrast with—or complement—the same character's *public behavior*. A memorable graphic version of this idea is a picture painted in gouache by the Belgian artist René Magritte in 1939. It shows the back of the head and shoulders of a man contemplating the ocean. The man's hair on the back of his head is parted, revealing a pair of eyes, a nose, and a mouth—the better to tell us what he might be contemplating in front. The painting is titled *The Glass House*, which is not as opaque a title as it would seem, or off the subject of acting either. The title is reminiscent of the story of Comus, the Greek god of mockery, who was unhappy that humans had no glass in their chests—the better for Comus to observe humans' whims.

In his novel *Tristram Shandy*, written in 1776, Laurence Sterne commiserates with Comus. If people were transparent, then all that the god or the writer (or, for that matter, any artist) would need to do to view or display a man's character was pull up a chair and watch:

> But this, as I said above, is not the case of the inhabitants of this earth; our minds shine not through the body, but are wrapt up here in a dark covering of uncrystalized flesh and blood; so that if we would come to the specifick characters of them, we must go some other way to work (90).

The man who seems to reveal his thoughts in Magritte's painting is as good as housed in glass. Just as transparently, characters in Shakespeare's plays report to the audience on their *inner* character.

Even committed villains turn out to have compunction, of sorts. The unscrupulous Richard III is alone with the audience when, waking from a nightmare, he admits his ambivalence:

RICHARD Alack, I love myself. Wherefore? For any good
　　That I myself have done unto myself?
　　O, no! Alas, I rather hate myself

TELLING A STORY

For hateful deeds committed by myself!
I am a villain: yet I lie, I am not.

Richard III, Act V, scene iii

Macbeth's introspection is part of his ambiguity, a brave man heroically facing up to the consequences of his cowardice.

MACBETH I have liv'd long enough: my way of life
Is fall'n into the sear, the yellow leaf;
And that which should accompany old age,
As honor, love, obedience, troops of friends,
I must not look to have . . .

Macbeth, Act IV, scene iii

While Shakespeare's soliloquies give actors access to a character's self-awareness, Molière's comedies include introspection as an opportunity to demonstrate the character's self-delusion. The story of a young bride seduced by a young man once the bride's elderly husband leaves town was familiar to Renaissance audiences from the improvisations of the Italian commedia dell'arte. This well-known scenario also occurs in Molière's *The School for Wives* (91), written in 1662, the year the playwright himself married a much younger woman. But Molière includes the episodes *within a story*: they are not shown, they are told.

The storyteller is Agnès, the young bride, who informs her older husband Arnolphe (played by Molière in the original production) just what has happened while Arnolphe was away:

AGNÈS It's the most amazing story you ever heard.
I was sewing, out on the balcony, in the breeze,
When I noticed someone strolling under the trees.
It was a fine young man, who caught my eye
And made me a deep bow as he went by.
I, not to be convicted of a lack
Of manners, very quickly nodded back.
At once, the young man bowed to me again.
I bowed to him a second time, and then
It wasn't very long until he made
A third deep bow, which I of course repaid.
He left, but kept returning, and as he passed,
He'd bow, each time, more gracefully than the last,
While I, observing as he came and went,
Gave each new bow a fresh acknowledgement.
Indeed, had night not fallen, I declare
I think that I might still be sitting there,

10

> And bowing back each time he bowed to me,
> For fear he'd think me less polite than he.
> ARNOLPHE Go on.
> AGNÈS Then an old woman came, next day,
> And found me standing in the entryway.
> She said to me, "May Heaven bless you, dear,
> And keep you beautiful for many a year.
> God, who bestowed on you such grace and charm,
> Did not intend those gifts to do men harm,
> And you should know that there's a heart which bears
> A wound which you've inflicted unawares."

The inner life of the character is revealed in this scene by the way the storyteller interprets what has happened. The events Agnès describes are different from the actual episode: THE YOUNG BRIDE DOESN'T KNOW SHE HAS BEEN SEDUCED. The audience takes pleasure in picturing this seduction while at the same time witnessing the rubber-faced husband's barely suppressed wrath and the naïve bride's seeming artlessness.

The past brought to the present in memory

Storytelling endures in the realistic theater, tucked within the framework of *memory*. As twentieth-century playwrights relied on the theory that past events explain present behavior, it became increasingly important to include memories onstage. No one has done this more consistently and effectively—or more beautifully—than the American playwright Tennessee Williams. The Mississippi-born playwright's southern heritage granted him direct experience of a culture haunted by memory and stories—the memory of losing a war, the stories of a long-gone glory.

In Williams's first important play, *The Glass Menagerie* (1944) (92), a character named Tom (the playwright's own nickname) walks onto the stage, like the Prologue in Plautus, and announces:

> TOM The play is memory. Being a memory play, it is dimly lighted, it is sentimental, it is not realistic. In memory everything seems to happen to music. That explains the fiddle in the wings.

From the opening speech, the audience is alerted that the realistic style of performance is an illusion that can be returned to or abandoned: *I am the narrator of the play, and also a character in it.*

Tom does take part in scenes; he also addresses the audience directly in monologues, all of them stories told from a point in time many years after the action of the play. There are memories within the scenes themselves, too, and they develop the dramatic action as strongly as dialogue or direct address. Amanda, the mother who dominates the family of *The Glass Menagerie*, has a fabled past, a fable she is glad to remember:

TELLING A STORY

> AMANDA One Sunday afternoon in Blue Mountain—your mother received—
> *seventeen!*—gentlemen callers! Why, sometimes there weren't chairs enough
> to accommodate them all . . .
> TOM How did you entertain those gentlemen callers?
> AMANDA I understood the art of conversation!

In this scene, Tom is not in the same room as his mother, Amanda, although Amanda speaks as if he were. As her story proceeds, Tom gives his cues, according to the stage direction: *as though reading from a script**—which is to say, not as emotionally involved as if he were fully in the scene. As Amanda continues her memory, the stage direction asks that:

> TOM *motions for music and a spot of light on* AMANDA. *Her eyes lift, her face glows, her voice becomes rich and elegiac.*

The story-telling actor separated from the scene by lighting, staging, or music is meant to transport a listening audience to the places he is describing. Williams used these techniques throughout his long career. The emotional range of the device can be as delicate as the violin-scored elegies in *The Glass Menagerie* or as melodramatic as the drums and cymbals in *Suddenly Last Summer* (1958). The latter is a single dramatic action comprising an entire play: the telling of a forbidden tale, itself a symbol, with cymbals. That awful pun is the least of the horrors in *Suddenly Last Summer*, which concludes with a twenty-minute monologue that climaxes, like a Greek tragedy, with the story of a man ripped to pieces by a mob.

One of the most powerful of memory stories occurs in Williams's *A Streetcar Named Desire* (1947) (94). The stage direction suggests that the speaker, Blanche, sit at a window sill, looking out. What it doesn't say, because it was considered too crass to mention, is that Blanche sits in the window so she may tell the story directly to the audience, while maintaining the realistic style of the performance.

> BLANCHE . . . When I was sixteen, I made the discovery—love. All at once
> and much, much too completely. It was like you suddenly turned a blind-
> ing light on something that had always been in shadow, that's how it struck
> the world for me. But I was unlucky. Deluded.

The speech is long. When the story it tells moves to a casino dance hall, the music Blanche remembers begins to play in the distance.

> BLANCHE We danced the Varsouviana! Suddenly in the middle of the dance
> the boy I had married broke away from me and ran out of the casino. A few
> moments later—a shot! I ran out—all did!—all ran and gathered about the

---

*These are the techniques of epic acting. Williams was a student at Piscator's Dramatic Workshop. After his first play was staged on Broadway, Williams asked to become Piscator's secretary. He was turned down; Piscator thought it more important for Williams to work on his own, although Williams did contribute to Piscator's 1942 staging of *War and Peace* (93).

terrible thing at the edge of the lake! I couldn't get near for the crowding. Then somebody caught my arm. "Don't go any closer! Come back! You don't want to see!"

The storyteller is, yes, sometimes reliving what she describes; the stage directions ask that she sway and cover her face, a gesture echoing what she would have done when she saw the body of her husband. But the storyteller does not remain in a state of emotional recall. Like Tom's monologues in *A Glass Menagerie*, the story is told from a vantage point several years later, when the character speaks with experience, not horror or shock.

> BLANCHE And then the searchlight which had been turned on the world was turned off again and never for one moment since has there been any light that's stronger than this—kitchen—candle . . .

A performer handed the gift of a Williams story to deliver has the chance to relive the events described, but also to plant in the audience's mind a scene that motivates the character's unending hunger for love. It is important that the audience picture that scene, even as they empathize with the character's pain or the emotional memory of the actress who is performing. Empathy and understanding are also the responsibility of the other actor onstage (playing Mitch, Blanche's would-be suitor) who, once Blanche has finished her tale, returns Blanche to the realistic world of the play by giving her a hug. Blanche stares at Mitch vacantly—her speech has lost any task related to him—until she too returns to the realism of the scene and, as the playwright asks, *huddles, sobbing in his embrace.*

Establishing the character in the world of the play

Among other playwrights, the American author Sam Shepard offers actors speeches that reveal how the roles they play acquire significance within the world of the play. This is done through descriptions—literally—of landscape, but also through moments of self-awareness. Such self-discovery would seem to be too private to enact. But, like the glory of the gods depicted by the Greeks or the introspection of Shakespeare's heroes, *self-discovery as storytelling* can be presented by an actor with precision and grace. This is from Shepard's Pulitzer Prize-winning play *Buried Child* (1978) (95):

> VINCE (*pause, delivers speech front*) I was gonna run last night. I was gonna run and keep right on running. I drove all night. Clear to the Iowa border. The old man's two bucks sitting right on the seat beside me. It never stopped raining the whole time. Never stopped once. I could see myself in the windshield. My face. My eyes. I studied my face. Studied everything about it. As though I was looking at another man. As though I could see his whole race behind him. Like a mummy's face. I saw him dead and alive at the same time. In the same breath. In the windshield, I watched him breathe as though he was frozen in time. And every breath marked him. Marked him forever without him knowing. And then his face changed. His face became his father's face. Same bones. Same eyes. Same nose. Same breath. And his father's face

changed to his Grandfather's face. And it went on like that. Changing. Clear on back to faces I'd never seen but still recognized. Still recognized the bones underneath. The eyes. The breath. The mouth. I followed my family clear into Iowa. Every last one. Straight into the Corn Belt and further. Straight back as far they'd take me. Then it all dissolved. Everything dissolved.

Buried Child is the story of the mysterious relations between a father, mother, and their two sons who live in a farmhouse similar to the cut-away rooms of O'Neill's *Desire Under the Elms*. Significantly, the upper story is unseen, just as the family's motives and desires are obscure. Vince is the only grandson of this family, and he hasn't seen them since he moved away from home. Now, he has returned, and he's brought his girlfriend along to meet his relations. But none of the family seem to recognize Vince or know who he is. In an effort, perhaps, to re-enter family life, Vince agrees to run an errand for his grandfather. Vince drives off, but takes so long to return that suspense builds with the possibility that he may have run away, leaving his girlfriend behind. This speech follows Vince's forceful return, which resembles an invasion when he rips through the screened porch and into the family home. The story itself is the revelation that, in the world of the play, Vince has fought his way back home for the highest good: to find his place in the family line.

Terms to Work with: Four Elements of Storytelling

No matter the play, an actor preparing to tell a story onstage should break a text down by separating four elements: *events, character quotes, descriptions*, and *story apparatus*. Each offers different opportunities for an actor and, if identified, each may be used in its own way to propel dramatic action.

At first, it helps to concentrate on answering the question of *HOW does the story mean?* before you go on to the equally important question of *WHAT does the story mean?* Working this way, you will begin by identifying the structure of the story before you decide on its meaning or interpretation.

In a better world, this could be called structural analysis, but let's use the term *narrative analysis* because the words *structural analysis* drag along implications—sometimes contradictory—piled on by linguists, anthropologists, psychologists, and literary critics. From Russia to Prague to Paris to Cambridge, Massachusetts, *structural analysts* of behavior, language, and culture have built up specialized vocabularies, none of them so far helpful to actors.

But at least one idea out of the structural analysis of literature is worth a performer's notice. In the late 1960s, a French critic named Jacques Derrida identified a process of separating a text into its parts—*deconstructing* is the jargon used—in order to recognize that meaning was relative and dependent on the reader—no matter what the intentions of the writer. Deconstructed, no text has a meaning without an organizing interpretation. Applied to a script, a performance text is broken down with an understanding that its meaning is subject to the way it is performed. This is the key concept for an actor to borrow from structuralism and deconstructivist theories.

For an actor to apply these concepts, it is necessary to rescue them from history and self-imposed obscurity by using clear, concise words in rehearsal and performance. Once more, let us agree to use a common vocabulary and proceed to the work of analyzing a variety of performance texts—by focusing on the aspects of a story that an actor can separate.

Event

An **event** is an episode that is described, not acted out. It is action that can be understood in and of itself, separately from its sequence. Events are the backbone of a story. A performer should usually begin preparation to tell an onstage story by first identifying events.

- I ran from the casino (from *A Streetcar Named Desire*).
- I saw a young man under my balcony (from *The School for Wives*).
- Our enemy sunk our ship (from *The Persians*).

Here is a sequence of three events from *Oedipus the King*: *We broke into the room. I saw the Queen. She was hanging from a rope.* Here is a sequence of two events from *Buried Child*, and in the words of the playwright: *I could see myself in the windshield. I studied my face.* Events are what you would like the audience to understand as happening—so that they may enact an episode in their mind's eyes. The events of the story, for the audience and for the performer, are understood in the sequence in which they are told, which is not always the sequence in which they happened.

Label events in the same way that you would label episodes. It helps to use complete sentences with subjects, verbs, and objects: *I walked into the room. I saw the woman. She saw me.* You can leave out the adjectives and the adverbs if you like. Answer the question: *Who did what to whom?* or *What happened?* In some cases the label will answer the question *What is happening now?* but the form of the answer is the same: a complete sentence.

The difference between an event and an episode is that an event is *described* and an episode is *enacted*. A sequence of events and their telling can very often become an episode onstage. For example, the sequence of events related by Agnès—*I was minding my business. I was distracted by a handsome young man. An old woman came to see me the next day*—create the episode: THE YOUNG BRIDE DOESN'T KNOW SHE HAS BEEN SEDUCED. Notice again that the episode is understood by the audience and the actor, but not necessarily by the character.

Character quotes

Stories often, though not always, include characters, including yourself, who act and speak in the course of the events. When a storyteller assigns a voice or gestures, or otherwise identifies a role within a story, this is a **character quote**:

- Then somebody caught my arm. "Don't go any closer! Come back! You don't want to see!"
- She said to me, "May Heaven bless you dear / And keep you beautiful for many a year."

TELLING A STORY

After you identify the events, you should identify the quotes. Answer the obvious questions: *Are there characters quoted? Who is quoted? How can the audience understand who these characters are?*

You can demonstrate how characters speak most simply by speaking in voices distinct from your own. The technique of quoting will be as familiar as telling a joke. Here's one from Samuel Beckett's *Endgame* (96):

> NAGG (*raconteur's voice*) An Englishman, needing a pair of striped trousers in a hurry for the New Year festivities, goes to his tailor who takes his measurements. (*tailor's voice*) "That's the lot, come back in four days, I'll have it ready." Good. Four days later. (*tailor's voice*) "So sorry, come back in a week, I've made a mess of the seat." Good, that's all right, a neat seat can be very ticklish. A week later. (*tailor's voice*) "Frightfully sorry, come back in ten days, I've made a hash of the crotch . . ."

There are more complications over details. Nagg ends his joke:

> NAGG Well, to make it short, the bluebells are blowing and he ballockses the buttonholes. (*customer's voice*) "God damn you to hell, Sir, it's indecent, there are limits! In six days, do you hear me, six days, God made the world. Yes, Sir, no less, Sir, the WORLD! And you are not bloody well capable of making me a pair of trousers in three months!" (*tailor's voice, scandalized*) "But my dear Sir, my dear Sir, look—(*disdainful gesture, disgustedly*)—at the world—(*pause*) and look—(*loving gesture, proudly*) at my TROUSERS!"

A character quote can be used even when there is no speech to quote in order to color emotionally the seemingly neutral *she says*, or a description of a character in a story:

> PALAESTRIO If you noticed, most of the hookers around here have twisted mouths. That's so they don't laugh in his face.

It's almost impossible not to say these lines without puckering up your mouth to demonstrate (and quote) the girls' attempts to keep a straight face.

The personification of characters within the story can be done with character-specific gestures or *physical quotes*; for example, the tailor's loving gesture toward his perfect trousers. A character quote does not have to be a fully embodied voice or pose; you can use very little. Even a shrug, if set up, will convey information about who is who. You can use a lot of details the first time a character is quoted, and fewer as the character reappears. Or the other way around: the character quote can build from slight details to a full personification. The only thing that's essential is that the audience knows who is speaking, especially if there are multiple voices and characters.

Sometimes, the character called *I* can be quoted, since *I*'s relationship to the speaker is not always direct. You may be describing yourself at an earlier age, or in a fantasy, or in an emotional state different from the one you are in while you are telling the story: "I was gonna run and keep right on running" is told by a narrator who has stopped running and returned to tell the story. The *I* of "I made the discovery—love" is different from the *I* of the experienced Blanche.

Within a character quote, a performer can apply actions to complete a task as well as utilize obstacles, transactions, and images. Set within a story, character quotes can display virtuoso realistic acting, but character quotes, like roles in episodes, shouldn't overwhelm the audience's understanding of events.

Descriptions

Descriptions are the words of a story that help the audience picture the events. Descriptions give meaning to action and behavior because they help to establish the world of the play, as it is presented in the story:

- Never stopped raining. Never stopped raining once.
- The sea was hidden, carpeted with wrecks / And dead men; all the shores and reefs were full of dead.
- The bluebells are blowing . . .

Descriptions can reflect the point of view of the character or of the narrator. They can set the emotional tone of the scene. Think of creaking doors, the dark of a corridor, the bright light of the heavens. All can be made to contribute to dramatic action with an image, but *not* by playing an action or a transaction.

Story apparatus

Story apparatus consists of the words in a story necessary for grammar, narrative devices, or the conventions of storytelling; conventions that call attention to the story as story:

- It's the most amazing story you ever heard . . .
- What happened after that I cannot tell . . .
- Think, when we talk of horses. That you see them . . .
- Well, to make it short . . .

The most frequent words of story apparatus are probably *she said, he said*. These can be made to do many things onstage. Among other things, they can give a story its bias or they can render the passage of time. The mechanical elements *she said, he said* can be inflected with a point of view. Agnès in *The School for Wives* continues her story:

> AGNÈS "You say I've wounded somebody?" I cried.
>   "Indeed you have," she said. "The victim's he
>   Whom yesterday you saw from the balcony."
>   "But how could such a thing occur?" I said;
>   "Can I have dropped some object on his head?"

Coloring the words "said" and "cried" will demonstrate *how* the quoted character did the saying. We hear these nuances in life when we listen to speakers, even when they are trying to be even-handed and impartial.

The words of story apparatus can be organized by tasks because they do have a job: *to make the story clear to the listeners*. The words of story apparatus can be thought of as transactions, too: *pay attention now / and you'll learn the important part.*

Each of the structural elements of a story presents its own options for an actor. Character quotes allow you to apply actions; descriptions do not. Character quotes and descriptions allow you to bring images to your preparation; story apparatus will not give you as much of a chance. Story apparatus will allow you to execute a task; events will not. This is not a matter of blind obedience to the writer's intentions; it is acceptance of the difficulty inherent in setting water on fire.

Analyzing a Story from *The School for Wives*

> AGNÈS It's the most amazing story you ever heard.

The story apparatus in this speech prepares Agnès's listeners—her husband Arnolphe and the audience—for what follows. These words can be given a task: *to get Arnolphe's help in explaining this mysterious stuff*, or *to share the wonder of an interesting day.*

> AGNÈS I was sewing, out on the balcony, in the breeze,
>   When I noticed someone strolling under the trees.

This is the only description in the text we are examining here, but it does set the emotional tone of what follows: breezy, carefree, and comfortably at home. The event described, which the audience, but not necessarily the character, is meant to understand: *I was minding my own business*. This is followed by the next event: *I was distracted by a handsome young man.*

> AGNÈS It was a fine young man, who caught my eye
>   And made me a deep bow as he went by.
>   I, not to be convicted of a lack
>   Of manners, very quickly nodded back.
>   At once, the young man bowed to me again.

There is the possibility of a character quote here by imitating the gesture of the young man's bow. There is also the possibility to quote yourself winking at the young man's advances. The next event: *His behavior confused me.*

> AGNÈS I bowed to him a second time, and then
>   It wasn't very long until he made
>   A third deep bow, which I of course repaid.
>   He left, but kept returning, and as he passed,

STORYTELLING

The next event: *I did the best I could to make sense of it.*

> AGNÈS He'd bow, each time, more gracefully than the last,
>   While I, observing as he came and went,
>   Gave each new bow a fresh acknowledgement.
>   Indeed, had night not fallen, I declare
>   I think that I might still be sitting there,

The words "I declare" are a little bit of story apparatus:

> AGNÈS . . . I declare
>   I think that I might still be sitting there,
>   And bowing back each time he bowed to me,
>   For fear he'd think me less polite than he.
> ARNOLPHE Go on.

Arnolphe is not telling a story, and his behavior may have the task *to control his emotions*, whether those emotions are fear, anger, or jealousy. His line can also be thought of as a transaction: *I'll keep my temper / you'll tell me what happened.* Meanwhile, the next event: *The next day, I learned what had happened*:

> AGNÈS Then an old woman came, next day,
>   And found me standing in the entryway.
>   She said to me, "May Heaven bless you, dear . . ."

This is a character quote and would be quite effective spoken in a very sweet and concerned voice. The image could be *a warning from a nun*.

> AGNÈS "And keep you beautiful for many a year.
>   God, who bestowed on you such grace and charm,
>   Did not intend those gifts to do men harm,
>   And you should know that there's a heart which bears
>   A wound which you've inflicted unawares."

To accomplish the task, the speaker will need *to warn, to protect, to twist, to seduce.* The frame of Agnès telling the story will prevent her from accurately quoting the old woman's real task: *to plant a seed of disquiet* in Agnès.

It is the work of another role to make the episode, and not just the events, clear:

> ARNOLPHE (*aside*) Old witch! Old tool of Satan! Damn her hide!

Arnolphe's lines might be said directly to the audience with the task *to warn the listener* not to trust what Agnès says about the old woman. The lines could also be considered part of the transaction with the audience: *In order to hear more / I will keep my thoughts to myself and the audience—but not my wife.*

AGNÈS "You say I've wounded somebody?" I cried.
"Indeed you have," she said. "The victim's he
Whom yesterday you saw from the balcony."
"But how could such a thing occur?" I said;
"Can I have dropped some object on his head?"

Agnès quoting herself can be done in such a way that the audience understands Agnès is an innocent girl who believes what she is told. The little scene between Agnès and the old woman will be organized by the old woman's task *to alarm the naïve girl* and Agnès' task *to apologize*. The image for the quote (and the episode) could very well be the innocent Marilyn Monroe of *Some Like It Hot*—or any other attractive woman unaware of the effect she has over men. If you like to use emotional memory, here's the place to do it: substitute a time from your past when you have made a social mistake unknowingly. The episode understood by the audience, but not the character: A MAN SEDUCED AGNES (AND SHE STILL DOESN'T REALIZE IT).

Let's Review Terms

To review: When you have a story that is supposed to stage the events it describes in the mind's eye of the listener, you should begin by separating four different elements.

events	episodes described in the story
character quotes	speaking or behaving in such a way as to identify characters who act or speak in the events of the story
description	the environment described in the story
story apparatus	words used as technical aspects of telling the story

The Chart

- **Appropriate playwrights.** It is appropriate to use these techniques whenever a story is told onstage. It is especially useful for plays by authors who rely on storytelling, rather than enactment, to create dramatic action on stage. These include the Greek playwrights, *Shakespeare*, *Bertolt Brecht*, *Tennessee Williams*, *Sam Shepard*, *Caryl Churchill*, and many others.
- **Intended reaction of the audience.** The audience is meant to *participate* in the creation of the action. By picturing it in their mind's eye they contribute to the dramatic events of the play.

Filling in the rest of the chart for a *Narrative Analysis*—illusion of character, dramatic action, key question—must wait. Separating the structural elements of a story is only part of the performer's task in preparing a story to be performed. There is more to be done, more questions to be answered.

CHAPTER 2

DRAMATIC ACTION AND ILLUSION OF CHARACTER

The Point of a Point of View

That cheerfully vulgar movie star Mae West, who wrote her own material, was brought to court several times for obscenity, but never in any trial could judge, juror, or prosecutor point to a single lascivious line. The Assistant District Attorney for the County of New York at Miss West's 1926 trial for performing, writing, and producing a play called—rather pointedly—*Sex* charged that "Miss West's personality, looks, walk, mannerisms and gestures made the lines and situations suggestive" (97).

Disappointed perhaps that Miss West did not demonstrate her belly dance (or what the prosecutor called her "danse du ventre"),* the jury nevertheless agreed with the assistant D.A., and at the height of her stage fame Mae spent eight days in the ladies' ward with two days off for good behavior. Even back in her vaudeville days, when she sang a little ditty called "The Cave Girl" (dressed in a leopard skin and, as she put it, singing the spots off it), Mae would conclude her act with a speech to the audience: "It isn't what I do, but how I do it. It isn't what I say, but how I say it, and how I look when I do it and say it" (98).

Once again, learn from Mae West: when you tell a story in a play, the illusion that you are someone other than yourself is created by the way you tell the tale. What you are talking about is not as important as how you talk about it. Not only do you have the power to characterize yourself in this way, the elements of a story—its events, character quotes, descriptions, and the apparatus of its telling—all change meaning depending on the **point of view** with which you present them to the audience. (In later years, Mae West used to end her act by reciting "Mary Had a Little Lamb"—with suggestive pauses.)

As another example of the way character can be revealed, think of an audience listening to a marriage announcement being read aloud by:

- the mother of the bride
- the bride's ex-boyfriend
- the girl who had a crush on the groom in high school

---

*Miss West hotly claimed these were innocent contractions of her abdominal muscles, an exercise learned from her athletic father.

- the groom's ex-wife
- the wedding editor at the newspaper who notices several grammatical mistakes
- the groom's mistress
- a radio announcer who doesn't know these people
- the bride

Change not a word, yet the meaning of the words will change with a change in perspective. Like Mae and Mary's lamb, an actor establishes character in storytelling by the intersection of the story and a point of view.

Points of View: Rehearsing a Monologue from *Buried Child*

Not every story has a characterized narrator. Some stories work without one: the description of the naval rout in *The Persians*, for example, reports the defeat without evoking a specific role or emotional reaction for the narrator. Storytelling without a characterized storyteller is common in Eastern theatrical traditions. There is also the genre in modern Western drama, called *Story Theater*, in which actors tell stories and recite stage directions and descriptions without any illusion that they are anything but performers. The use of story apparatus—*she said, then it happened, one day it happened*—further identifies Story Theater performers as actors, not characters.

Story Theater occasionally has its uses for a characterized monologue, but not often. The switch from enactment to narrative offers a wide range of expression, and has been used successfully to stage novels as sweeping as Dickens's *Nicholas Nickleby* and John Steinbeck's *The Grapes of Wrath*. But when the choice is made to characterize the narrator, there are usually four categories of points of view from which to choose. Each requires the collaboration of the audience to establish the illusion that the speaker is a person distinct from the story-telling actor.

Identification

When the narrator **identifies** with the story being told, the words of the text are meant to be understood as a faithful description of the speaker's emotional state, and the actor is meant to use the power of images to persuade the audience that the description is true.

> VINCE I could see myself in the windshield. My face. My eyes. I studied my
> face. Studied everything about it. As though I was looking at another man.
> As though I could see his whole race behind him. Like a mummy's face.

If the actor playing Vince identifies with the lines, he will take the time to recreate the moment of being transfixed by his own reflection. If successful, Vince's rapture will be understood by the audience much more clearly than if the actor were sitting onstage under a spotlight in a rolled-on car seat and gripping one of those cliché fragments of a steering wheel. It helps that the speech is written in the first person, using the word *I*.

But *I* doesn't always have to be present for there to be identification. The feeling of exaltation in communion with one's family will be understood by the audience in this description without the use of the word *I*—if the actor chooses to make it so.

> VINCE And then his face changed. His face became his father's face. Same
> bones. Same eyes. Same nose. Same breath. And his father's face changed
> to his Grandfather's face.

Emotional identification with the story can extend to the act of speaking itself. This story is being told by someone who ran away from his home and his roots. The act of speaking is the act of rejoining them.

> VINCE I followed my family clear into Iowa. Every last one.

The statement is a vow of commitment. The actor's sincerity will persuade the audience that the story he is telling—about his feelings—is accurate and true, and that he has returned.

Bias

When the narrator speaks with **bias** about the story being told, the audience is meant to synthesize the meaning of the text and the narrator's point of view to establish for themselves the character of the narrator and the nature of events. Skepticism, sarcasm, favoritism, outrage, and shame are all attitudes with which to tell a biased story. The audience should understand the narrator's bias, although they don't have to agree with it.

The story from *Buried Child* begins with the following lines:

> VINCE I was gonna run last night. I was gonna run and keep right on running.
> I drove all night. Clear to the Iowa border. The old man's two bucks sitting right on the seat beside me.

This part of the story can be told in such a way that we know the speaker thinks running is useless. In life, the emotions evoked by memory don't necessarily repeat what the person felt at the time it happened. Vince's adolescent rebellion is spoken of by a more mature man. The way Vince tells the story now tells the audience who he has become since the events described.

A critical narrator speaks with bias in description, character quotes, events, and even story apparatus. When the presumably English Chorus of *Henry V* describes the French, he does so critically. So does the servant who describes his master's excesses, or the villain describing the hero—or a good deed.

The bias of criticism isn't always negative. An actor can tell a story biased with approval. When Brecht noticed Helene Weigel performing the Servant's speech from *Oedipus the King*, what struck Brecht was the Servant's grudging admiration for death, in opposition to her concern for her mistress. Agnès's understanding of her story in

The School for Wives is at odds with what she is describing, and even if she doesn't know it, the audience does, and it characterizes her point of view as naïve (although this naïveté might be an equally characteristic pose on the part of the ingenue).

Distanced point of view

When a story is told with a **distanced** point of view, the storyteller tries to keep personal bias out of the story. When stories are written in the third person, the performer may speak with the distance of an uninvolved observer, even ludicrously, as when a cheery television announcer reports a disaster.

A distanced point of view can even be used for stories that are written in the first person using the word *I*. When an actor speaks of intimate details with the objectivity of a third-person point of view, this invites the audience to create the illusion of a character for the speaker. The audience tends to assign motives for objectivity: the speaker is in shock, or callous, or forgiving, or that much more heroic for facing the truth about himself. This would be the case if Vince switched from identification to a more distanced point of view at the end of his story:

> VINCE I followed my family clear into Iowa. Every last one. Straight into the Corn Belt and further. Straight back as far as they'd take me. Then it all dissolved. Everything dissolved.

The building rhythm of the lines "Straight into the Corn Belt and further. Straight back as far they'd take me" suggests *identification*, and the changed rhythm of "Then it all dissolved"—as well as the new event and subject matter—suggests a distanced approach on the last words: "Everything dissolved."

In the same speech from *Buried Child*, there are passages of *description* that are told very naturally from a distanced point of view.

> VINCE I drove all night. Clear to the Iowa border. The old man's two bucks sitting right on the seat beside me. It never stopped raining the whole time. Never stopped once.

If that same distanced point of view was applied to the whole speech, the audience would still understand the events of the story, but would probably not gain as much insight into the character of the speaker. Sometimes a distanced point of view is meant to supplement the illusion of character, in the same way a Cubist painter shows the profile of the same face that's being depicted head-on. Such a use of a distanced point of view—essentially a report to the audience from the actor—can be used to isolate behavior and call attention to it outside of its context, the process Brecht called *alienation*.

Brecht was a master of using a distanced point of view to describe highly emotional situations. In his early play *Drums in the Night* (1922) (99), a young girl, pregnant and engaged, tells her ex-boyfriend what has happened while he was away in Africa soldiering:

ANNA In the beginning you were with me a long time, your voice was still fresh. When I went down the hall, I brushed against you, and out in the meadow you called me from behind the maple tree. Even though they wrote that you'd been shot through the face and buried two days later. But then one day it was different. When I went down the hall, it was empty, and the maple tree didn't speak. When I stood up from bending over the wash trough, I still saw your face, but when I spread the washing out on the grass, I didn't see it, and all that time I didn't know what you looked like. But I should have waited.

The whole story, start to finish, can be told icily, with as distanced a point of view as possible. Let the audience assign the emotions here, and they will. You could even smoke while you said it.

There is no episode (since nothing changes onstage) until the soldier, Kragler, speaks:

KRAGLER You should have had a picture.
ANNA I was afraid. Even with my fear I should have waited, but I'm no good. Let go of my hand, everything about me is bad.

If Kragler says his line gently, tenderly feeling sorry for Anna, the episode will become HE FORGIVES HER. If he is angry at himself, the episode will be something else. If he is as distanced as Anna, the episode will wait until he lets go of her hand, which will then become the *gest*.

Projection

When an actor telling a story **projects** onto the audience a response that influences the telling of the story, the audience is cast in a role and both the speaker and his listeners are characterized. This can happen in a realistic play when the convention of the fourth wall allows the audience to be addressed as, say, a crowd or a school-room of students. In less realistic plays, soliloquies and prologues and asides may be openly spoken to the audience as audience. When the audience is effectively cast as a partner, a relationship of tasks and actions—or transactions and *gests*—now extends beyond the fourth wall to establish interaction between performers and listeners.

Although the script doesn't specify it, some of the lines from the speech we are looking at from *Buried Child* could be delivered directly to a *characterized audience*.

VINCE His face became his father's face. Same bones. Same eyes. Same nose. Same breath. And his father's face changed to his Grandfather's face. And it went on like that. Changing. Clear on back to faces I'd never seen but still recognized. Still recognized the bones underneath. The eyes. The breath. The mouth.

The actor playing Vince could look at the audience members as if they were the faces he described. He could establish a line of them in the audience, one behind the other. For each face he could attempt the task *to find myself*. His obstacles would be the change in noses and eyes and other features; the action would be *to search each face* until he did see some resemblance. The conclusion of the task, his reunion with his ancestors, is dictated by the words of the text; whatever the audience's real response, the response necessary for the story would be projected by the storyteller onto his listeners.

In life, the reactions of the audience shift and change, just as any other partner's do. It is the actor's choice to interpret the audience's changing reactions as approval or disapproval, and sometimes, in the absence of spectators, to imagine that someone is reacting. Improvisers can change what they say to respond to the audience. Performers who honor the words of the text by speaking them as written can still alter *the meaning* of those words in order to respond.

Sometimes the audience can be coaxed into playing their part. Sometimes they offer themselves a little too enthusiastically. When Stanislavsky played Dr. Stockman in Ibsen's *An Enemy of the People* in 1904, the play's protests against corrupt authority were recognized by the Russian audience as references to their own country's sorry politics. The Tsar's censor sat backstage at every performance to make sure that only an approved and censored script was spoken. The production opened in St. Petersburg on the night of a massacre in that town, and during the performance the audience broke into pandemonium. In character as Dr. Stockman, Stanislavsky had lines to say like "I'll cry out the truth from every street corner! The whole country will learn what's happened!" The stage was low, and there was no orchestra pit; hundreds of spectators reached across the footlights to shake hands with Stanislavsky, as if he were Dr. Stockman. Some audience members jumped onto the stage and embraced him (100).

But Stanislavsky understood that the task of his role was *to search for truth*. Any popular acclamation was an obstacle to the actor and to the character he played. The admiration of the crowd, characterized in this way, was such a living presence that it egged Stanislavsky on to speak the words of the text with fury and purpose.

> "You are mistaken, you are animals, yes animals," I said to the crowd at the public lecture in the fourth act of the play, and I said this truthfully and sincerely, for I was able to assume the viewpoint of Stockman himself. And I found it pleasant to say this to feel that the spectator, who had begun to love me in the role of Stockman, was excited and angry at me for the tastelessness of arousing my enemies with too much sincerity (101).

As an active partner, as a listener who deduces motivation, or as a spectator convinced by passion, the audience collaborates with an actor telling a story to create the illusion of character.

The Shifting Point of View

While telling a story, a **shift in the point of view** is dramatic action. When any actress playing Amanda in *The Glass Menagerie* warms herself with the memory of her girlhood ("*seventeen* gentlemen callers!"); when the actor telling the tale of the tailor in *Endgame* cracks himself up laughing ("and look, Sir, at my trousers!"); when *An Enemy of the People*'s Dr. Stockman turns on the crowd; then the episode onstage is that *change* in the storyteller. This is not always the progression of the events described.

Just as every story told onstage doesn't necessarily have a characterized narrator, not every story has a dramatic action. If there is a progression of events with no change in the teller, that might be dramatic if the events described were interesting. But it is not active. This can be exactly what is called for in, say, a bulletin or a report. Here the dramatic action is meant to be in the audience's mind, not in the performance of the play.

This is the difference between reciting and acting. When dramatic poetry is recited, the words themselves will evoke pictures for the audience to animate. This lack of dramatic action sometimes happens during performances of arias in operas. The progression of music is, for some listeners and singers, theater enough. Sometimes, when an actor achieves an unvarying emotional tone, there is no action, just emotion. This is permissible in a film performance, which can be edited to create action by alternating the point of view of the camera, if not the speaker.

To identify a change or changes in the point of view onstage, it helps to look at what is different about the narrator at the beginning of the story compared to the narrator at the end. The question to ask is: *What happens to the teller while telling the story?*

The most familiar shift in point of view, due to the conventions of realism (not life), is when an actor begins with a *distanced* point of view and moves slowly in degrees to *identification*, ultimately reliving the event at the moment of its description. There are many other possibilities, however. Let's look again at the text from *Buried Child*:

> VINCE (*pause, delivers speech front*) I was gonna run last night. I was gonna run
>   and keep right on running . . .

The speaker begins with a biased point of view: what a foolish thing it was to try to run away. Then the point of view shifts to a more distanced observation. The *I* of the story is seen objectively, without bias.

> VINCE I drove all night. Clear to the Iowa border. The old man's two bucks
>   sitting right on the seat beside me. It never stopped raining the whole time.
>   Never stopped once.

Emotional identification begins. The *I* is the speaker, reliving a past event. This is by no means the only way to interpret these lines, but let's choose it as a way to quote behavior.

VINCE I could see myself in the windshield. My face. My eyes. I studied my face. Studied everything about it. As though I was looking at another man. As though I could see his whole race behind him. Like a mummy's face. I saw him dead and alive at the same time. In the same breath. In the windshield, I watched him breathe as though he was frozen in time. And every breath marked him. Marked him forever without him knowing. And then his face changed.

Emotional identification could continue here, or as discussed above, the actor could *project* the story onto the audience. The faces lined up behind each other would be cast as the generations of ancestors.

VINCE His face became his father's face. Same bones. Same eyes. Same nose. Same breath. And his father's face changed to his Grandfather's face. And it went on like that. Changing. Clear on back to faces I'd never seen but still recognized. Still recognized the bones underneath. The eyes. The breath. The mouth.

The actor could interpret the audience's reaction as distrust, followed by acceptance. Emotional identification could return to a declaration:

VINCE I followed my family clear into Iowa. Every last one. Straight into the Corn Belt and further. Straight back as far they'd take me. Then it all dissolved.

The story could now be told from a more distanced point of view that would parallel the events of the story: *Everything dissolved.* The episode: VINCE REJOINS HIS FAMILY. The events, baldly put, are:

- *Vince ran away from home.*
- *As he drove, he studied his own face.*
- *He had a vision of himself as part of a family line.*
- *He returned home.*

The dramatic action of the story is the change in the point of view:

- Biased point of view: *I was gonna run . . .*
- Distanced observation: *Never stopped raining . . .*
- Emotional identification: *I could see my face . . .*
- Projected story onto the audience: *My father's face . . .*
- Emotional identification: *I followed my family . . .*
- Distanced point of view: *It all dissolved . . .*

The change in the speaker is from scorn to acceptance. This, of course, is an interpretation, and other interpretations are possible. What stays the same are the events, and the episode itself.

Some playwrights dictate changes in the point of view while stories are being told. In Eugene O'Neill's *Strange Interlude* (102), the characters speak their thoughts aloud. Here are the stage directions the playwright set down for a single character thinking aloud for the first three pages of text:

- *His voice takes on a monotonous musing quality, his eyes stare idly at his drifting thoughts*
- *He smiles*
- *His face has become sad with a memory of the bewildered suffering of [an] adolescent boy*
- *He shakes his head, flinging off his thoughts*
- *He sighs—then self-mockingly*
- *Then self-reassuringly*
- *He grins torturedly*
- *His face suddenly full of an intense pain and disgust*
- *Mocking bitterly*
- *Impatiently*

A performer who abides by these stage directions accepts O'Neill's attempt to make dramatic action out of the shift in the point of view. It almost works, but the play is nine acts long and the running time usually exceeds the patience of an audience. The gossip goes that when the script was first produced, the producers begged O'Neill to make cuts. He was very resistant. One day he called them up to say that he had figured out a way to cut an hour and a half from the performance. They were very happy, until O'Neill told them his idea was to cut the lunch and dinner breaks.

In O'Neill's masterpiece, *Long Day's Journey into Night*, the climax of the play is the mother's story of how she came to leave her school and marry. In order for this long speech to be logically included in the realistic style of the play, it is framed as an opium-induced regression to an earlier identity. O'Neill specifies that Mary begin listlessly and that her voice take on a young quality as she moves further into her tale. Because he is writing a realistic play, O'Neill must explain this transformation as the effect of the narcotic. Explained by medicine or not, the metamorphosis is magical and powerfully moving: out of the body of a life-shattered old woman rises a young girl filled with hope.

In the film version of *Long Day's Journey into Night* (1962) directed by Sidney Lumet, the body of the speech is performed by Katharine Hepburn in one long take. The camera echoes her drifting romantic point of view by slowly ascending high above the room. From close-up to panorama, the camera lifts back from the actors' faces, to the table where they sit, to the shadowy room, until at last the shot widens so far that what is seen on screen resembles what an audience member would see watching a play, not a film, in a theater. The actors are dwarfed by the black surround, no longer providing information to illustrate the scene; the audience must concentrate on the words being spoken to picture what is being described.

Then, when Hepburn speaks the last line, the camera cuts to a sharp and startling close-up so as to parallel the reversion in the storyteller's point of view from hope to experience. Usually in a film monologue like this, footage would be pieced together and therefore unreliable as evidence of a performance, but Sidney Lumet wanted the film *Long Day's Journey into Night* to resemble a stage play in process as well as technique.* The actors had three weeks' rehearsal, the shoot was short—less than forty days—and most generously, it was filmed in sequence, Hepburn's monologue included.

As convoluted as a plot, or as simple as a fall off a cliff, movement of the point of view creates dramatic action, which distinguishes storytelling in a play from recitation.

Let's Review Terms

point of view	the storyteller's reaction to the story being told
distanced point of view	the storyteller remains impartial while telling the story
identification	the storyteller emotionally identifies with the story being told
biased point of view	the storyteller comments on the story being told
projection onto the audience	the storyteller characterizes a listening audience
shift in the point of view	a change in the storyteller's attitude as the story is told

The Chart

- **Basic unit.** The *event* and the *point of view* are the basic units in storytelling.
- **Illusion of character.** The illusion of character for a storyteller is the *intersection of point of view and the story*.
- **Dramatic action.** A *shift in the point of view* of the storyteller creates dramatic action.
- **Key question.** There are two key questions for telling a story onstage: *What am I describing?* and *What's my point of view about it?*
- **Unifying image.** The unifying image of telling a story is the *film camera's use of different angles* to show the same event or object.

---

*Although Lumet couldn't resist adding a reverb to Hepburn's voice to heighten the sense of distance. Hepburn derived her mannerisms for this performance from an image of her own mother.

- **Relative theory.** A model for storytelling onstage can be derived from the theories of *literary deconstruction* that the meaning of a text is determined by the reader—and creative actor.

Switching from Acting to Storytelling: Rehearsing a Scene from *Iphigenia in Aulis*

You don't need to restrict narrative analysis to monologues; the techniques used to tell a story can be applied to scenes. Certain playwrights give an actor artful possibilities to switch from narrative to demonstration. Some of the greatest opportunities are in texts written by Shakespeare, Brecht, and Euripides, the third of the great Greek playwrights. Let's use as an example a scene with two long stories from the last play Euripides wrote, *Iphigenia in Aulis* (103).

The play takes place during the Trojan War. The Greek fleet is stalled in Aulis, becalmed on its way to Troy and waiting for a wind. Agamemnon (pronounced a-ga-MEM-non) is the elected commander of the fleet. He has agreed to sacrifice his daughter Iphigenia (if-e-je-NY-a *or* if-e-je-NEE-a) in order to convince the gods to send a wind to move the fleet. But Agamemnon has thought more deeply about killing his own child and has sent a letter to his wife telling her not to come with Iphigenia. Agamemnon's brother, Menelaus (me-ne-LAY-us) has confiscated the letter and is outraged that Agamemnon has gone back on his word. Before the play starts, Menelaus's wife Helen has run away with a Trojan prince. It is to recapture Helen from Troy that the Greek fleet led by Agamemnon is assembled in Aulis. Each brother accuses the other of a conflict of personal and political interests.

The example is long and difficult to read—which is the reason to read it. The impulse otherwise is to cut so much talk, because the performer (or director) does not understand how it can be made dramatic. Be patient. The first time you read a story this complicated is similar to a first rehearsal when dialogue is obscure and the character of the roles unknown. To save time and energy at rehearsals, narrative analysis can—and should—start with the actor at home. In rehearsal you can test your ideas, revise them, refine them, abandon them if they don't work, and try others. As before, what follows is one interpretation of the scene; other interpretations are possible.

The scene begins with the brothers confronting each other over the letter Agamemnon has tried to send to his wife, taking back his promise to sacrifice his daughter.

AGAMEMNON So, you have broken the seal [of my letter] and read it. It was not for your eyes.

MENELAUS Yes, I read it. I know your secrets and your shame. You will regret it.

AGAMEMNON Gods above! The arrogance of the man! Where did you waylay my messenger?

MENELAUS I was waiting for your daughter to come here from Argos.

AGAMEMNON Why?

MENELAUS Because I felt like it. I am not your slave.

AGAMEMNON This is an outrage. Am I not to be master of my own house?

MENELAUS Not when you are a cheat and a liar, when you slither your way into everything.

AGAMEMNON You talk to me of cheating and of lying. You! I hate a facile, quick tongue.

First identify episodes and events

The backbone of a story—and a scene—is *what happens*. As you read the text, establish episode and event first, and, in separating storytelling from enactment, distinguish between episodes shown onstage and events that are described.

The episode is MENELAUS CATCHES HIS SUCCESSFUL OLDER BROTHER IN THE WRONG. The dialogue can be played for tasks and actions. Agamemnon's super-task will be *to save his daughter's life*; his first task will be *to brush off his brother's accusations*. The obstacles will be *the oath* he swore before and *the letter* in his brother's hand. Menelaus's super-task will be *to repossess his wife*. The obstacle will be *Agamemnon's compunction* about sacrificing his daughter. Menelaus's action will be *to rebuke Agamemnon*, which will run up against the next obstacle, the *successful politician's poise*.

MENELAUS And I hate a devious, quick mind.

Menelaus could say this to Agamemnon, but he could also say it to the audience, *projecting* onto the listeners the identity of Greeks. The original audiences for this play were accustomed to personal address. They were the same group who voted on political issues of state and to whom speakers pleaded with sentiments similar to the lines of the play. Menelaus's task here could be *to persuade the listeners* to agree with him. The obstacle would be *their respect for Agamemnon* as their commander.

What follows is story apparatus. It reveals the speaker's bias for the story that is to follow. It also sets up the beginning of the episode: HOT-HEADED MENELAUS PROMISES NOT TO PUSH HIS ARGUMENT. The words of the story apparatus have a task too: *to expose his brother in public*.

MENELAUS You know neither justice nor honesty. I will prove your guilt. No lies, my brother! No quick denials. You cannot bluff your way out of this. Listen to me. I will not be too hard on you.

This is followed by an event: *When Agamemnon wanted to be elected commander, he bribed the Greeks with condescension.*

MENELAUS Do you remember your past ambitions? To be leader of the Greeks against Troy? You pretended to be reluctant. But in your heart you longed for it. And to get it you groveled. You shook everyone by the hand. Your doors were open to all who wished to enter. You spoke to everyone, whether they wanted to listen or not. You were nice to everyone. You wanted to be popular. You wanted no rivals.

After events are established, you can assign character quotes

Character quotes relate to events as roles in an episode. Once the event is established, if the text allows, you may add a character quote. Even if there are no spoken words to quote, as is the case here, you could quote: "You shook everyone by the hand. Your doors were open to all who wished to enter. You spoke to everyone, whether they wanted to listen or not. You were nice to everyone" demonstrating with an outstretched hand and plastered-on smile the behavior of a solicitous and oily politician. Notice that within the quote, you have the task of getting elected by the voters. The character quote of the concerned politician Agamemnon switches here to the biased narrator Menelaus, whose task is *to mock his brother*. Bias can be established by the way "nice" is spoken.

The second event is announced: *When Agamemnon got what he wanted, he was his same old standoffish self.*

> MENELAUS But then when you were made commander-in-chief, you changed your tune. You abandoned all your old friends. You were inaccessible. You locked your doors. You rarely appeared in public.

After episodes and events, identify the changes in point of view

Because the dramatic action of telling the story is created by a change in the point of view, once events and episodes are clarified, the next step is to see how the perspective of the story changes. Here, Menelaus shifts from speaking to Agamemnon to speaking to the audience. This will be a powerful dramatic action; Menelaus's task will still be *to win the listeners to his opinion*, just as he would in a political debate. First, he speaks to his brother.

> MENELAUS Brother, a good man does not change when he gets on in the world.

Then Menelaus might speak to the audience:

> MENELAUS That is precisely the time when his friends ought to be able to count on him, when his power and success allow him to do more for them than ever.

Story apparatus follows:

> MENELAUS This is my first point, my first reproach—your lack of character.

Story apparatus often has a task; here it is *to alert the listeners* to the pattern of Agamemnon's wrongdoing. Framed by this biased point of view, the next event is stated: *A crisis came and Agamemnon was paralyzed.*

> MENELAUS Then, when the Greek army came here to Aulis and we were denied a favoring wind, you became the lowest of the low. This injunction of the gods filled you with fear. The Greeks shouted at you, demanded that the fleet turn back, that you put an end to this futile delay.

Within the quote, establish tasks or transactions

The event sets the stage in the audience's minds for the character quote that follows, developed slowly—first face, then voice.

> MENELAUS One could see the distress on your face. You could not bear the thought of not launching your thousand ships, of not filling the fields of Troy with the cries of war. So you came to me. "What shall I do? How can I get out of this?" You were afraid of losing your command, losing the glory.

Rather than play bewildered—a vague state of emotion—it will help the character quote ("What shall I do? How can I get out of this?") if it is an action—*to beg*—done to fulfil a task: *to rescue his command.* The quote can also be organized as a transaction: *Agamemnon will humble himself, even ask advice / if Menelaus will help him.*

> MENELAUS Then Calchas [the head priest] spoke. You were to sacrifice your daughter. Only then would the Greeks be free to sail to Troy. You were quick to make promises. And your heart smiled. No one forced you to do what you did next. You cannot say that. You sent word to your wife that your daughter was to come to Aulis and be married to Achilles. That was the pretext you devised. And now?

Story apparatus helps to establish the point of view

The story apparatus—"And now?"—reinforces the bias that these events add up to the pattern of Agamemnon's duplicity. The speaker loses his temper, which is a change in the point of view from distance to identification:

> MENELAUS And now? You have been caught red-handed. You have changed your mind and sent a different message.

A quote follows. In some translations it is a direct quote: "I am no longer . . . prepared to be my daughter's killer." It might be more effective, in this translation, to display the words with a distanced bias, even distaste, rather than to directly quote them:

> MENELAUS You are no longer prepared to be your daughter's killer.

If the speaker addressed the rest to the personified audience of Greeks, a new task—*to egg his listeners on to condemn Agamemnon*—would organize the story apparatus that follows:

> MENELAUS I cannot be more blunt. This is the same heaven that bore witness to your oaths.

The obstacle for Menelaus is that *the audience doesn't take sides*. This could anger him, and the dramatic action would be his increasing identification with what he is saying:

> MENELAUS Think! You are not unique. Many a man has worked hard to gain power. And many a man has lost that power in shame. Sometimes it is the fault of the people. They do not understand the complexity of power. But just as often it is the man himself who is incompetent and fails to protect the interests of the people.

The telling of the story should be an episode

So that an episode happens onstage and not just in the minds of the audience, a change should come over the speaker as he tells his tale. Here, Menelaus, who began speaking with a promise to remain calm, loses his temper: YOUNGER BROTHER LOSES HIS TEMPER AT SUCCESSFUL OLDER BROTHER. What he says next is petty and pointed:

> MENELAUS My tears are for Greece. She planned an action steeped in glory. Now she must suffer the mockery of barbarians. All because of you and your daughter. It is not courage that makes a great leader or a great general. It is intelligence. A man who has half a brain can be governor of a state. But a commander-in-chief must be blessed with intelligence.

Still speaking to the audience, personified as the Greek army, Menelaus might choose a task *to arouse the Greeks to strip his brother of command*. The obstacle will remain that the army respects Agamemnon—and has lost respect for Menelaus.

You can refer to the world of the play

This play is set on a battlefield. The rules of the world of this play are those of army life. Self-control is strength, losing one's temper is weakness. Status is based on rank, but also on public displays of strength. A public display of spite will lose Menelaus status. Loyalty—including loyalty to one's family and loyalty to one's brother—is ranked as a high good in this play.

CHORUS When brothers fight and anger and recrimination fly between them,
there is only sorrow.

The single line of the Chorus, if it is not to become a throw-away line, should be given importance as an episode: THE CHORUS BALANCES THE ATTACK ON THE COMMANDER WITH THE RULES OF THE WORLD.

The Chorus is a group of women come from another city to watch the Greek fleet. This is not a matter of opinion or costume; the Chorus Leader identifies herself to the audience in direct words: "I have come to the shore and the sands of Aulis . . . from Chalcis, my city . . . to see this fleet." It's possible to direct this scene so that Agamemnon and Menelaus are trying to persuade the Chorus, not the audience, but this might make the leaders of the Greek army look silly, as if they were playing to groupies from another town. It might be more dramatic if it is the audience, personified as the Greek army, who must be convinced.

Even so, the response of the Chorus needs to be given weight as its own episode, and in the role of judge. What is the morality of keeping a bad promise? What is the morality of abiding by a bad treaty? The use of dueling stories helps Euripides keep his evaluation of morality open-ended, unfinished, and relative. Euripides presents several points of view, none correct, echoing the erosion of values at the time he was writing.

The one thing the playwright does insist on is that the old certainty of a single narrative is gone. Euripides tells another version of Iphigenia's story in his play *Iphigenia in Tauris* (104), which includes this speech:

ORESTES Even the gods who claim to see the future are as blind as we.
In heaven, as on earth, confusion reigns.

Iphigenia in Tauris

Iphigenia in Aulis was Euripides's last play, written and staged during a Civil War so corrupting that a contemporary historian recorded that even "words had to change their ordinary meaning and take that which was now given them" (105). The lines in the play that question the meaning of honor, loyalty, and truth echo a contemporary political debate—contemporary then and contemporary now.

The telling of the story can be dramatic action

Agamemnon's reply to Menelaus sets his story against his brother's, but even more, sets his own calm point of view against his brother's hot-headedness. The story apparatus is tempered with a deliberately distanced point of view.

AGAMEMNON Now it is my turn to criticize you. I will be compassionate, not
arrogant. I will show you the respect due a brother.

Even his address to the audience advises temperance.

DRAMATIC ACTION AND ILLUSION OF CHARACTER

AGAMEMNON Compassion springs from a good heart.

The original audience for *Iphigenia in Aulis* would have understood, and, by force of habit, participated in the evaluation of Menelaus and Agamemnon's opinions. Caught up in their own ongoing civil war, they were voting on policies after public discussions not unlike those in the play—including debates on honoring bad promises. Directing these lines to the audience, telling the stories rather than enacting them, will return a structure to the text of *Iphigenia* that makes the play in performance dramatic and interesting.

As a distanced narrator, Agamemnon will not use character quotes to describe his brother and establish the event: *Menelaus began all this because he couldn't keep his wife at home*.

> AGAMEMNON Tell me first why you are so angry. You are short of breath, your face is flushed. Why? Who has done you wrong? What do you want? Do you desire to win yourself a good wife? I cannot help you there. You had no control over the one you had. *You* made the mistakes. Must *I* pay for them? *I* do not have an adulteress for a wife. You talk of my ambition. But it is not *that* which torments you. No. You long to hold a beautiful woman in your arms. Discretion and common decency mean nothing to you. Your passions make you grovel. You have become an evil man.

Agamemnon will try to persuade the audience that he is acting for impersonal reasons, not just to save his daughter's life.

> AGAMEMNON If I have the intelligence to undo a previous mistake—am I to be called a fool? You are the fool. You lost a faithless wife and now you want her back—be the gods willing.

The story that follows alternates its focus between Menelaus and the listening army. Speaking to his brother, Agamemnon's task will be *to rebuke Menelaus*; speaking to the audience, Agamemnon will appeal to the common sense of people in a similar crisis—as was true when the play was first performed.

> AGAMEMNON Think back. The suitors who pursued Helen swore all manner of oaths to her father. But *you* won her hand. Not through strength or virtue but by the help of a goddess—the goddess of Hope. You want an army? Conscript the suitors! Be their general! They were fools before, why not now?

A shift in the point of view takes the distanced Agamemnon to identification with what he is saying:

> AGAMEMNON But the gods are not fools. They know when an oath has been sworn under duress and when a promise is evil.

37

TELLING A STORY

As identified storyteller, using the word *I* and identifying with it emotionally, Agamemnon can speak passionately here, and with great force.

> AGAMEMNON I will not kill my child. Why should you, with no concern for what is right, take vengeance on a worthless wife and live a life of happiness and success while I am forced to weep unending tears for my sins, my unjust unconscionable sins against my own child? I shall say no more. I have been brief and to the point. If you will not see sense, that is your choice. But I must follow my conscience and do what I must do.

Agamemnon, for at least this part of the play, joins other characters written by Euripides who defy conventional loyalty and denounce the honor of war as dishonorable. The speaking of the lines is the *gest* of an episode:

AGAMEMNON PUBLICLY GOES BACK ON HIS PROMISE

The Chorus tries to stay neutral, balancing the alternative points of view.

> CHORUS Your words have changed—for the better. You now refuse to harm your child.

But Menelaus is hot-headed. To his mind, the listeners are either for him or against him.

> MENELAUS Then I am alone. I have no friends.

Rather than say this line sarcastically or reproachfully to the Chorus—would Menelaus really be that concerned over the opinion of some women from Chalcis?—it might work just as well to say it to the audience. Menelaus will be just as biased but without the added blinders of pettiness. The scene then switches from storytelling to dialogue.

> AGAMEMNON Not true. Simply stop destroying the friends that you have.
> MENELAUS Are you our father's son!? Prove it!
> AGAMEMNON We should be brothers in virtue, not in sin.
> MENELAUS If you *were* my friend, you would share in my misfortunes.
> AGAMEMNON Brother, you hurt me. If you chastise me, do it with some good in mind.
> MENELAUS Are you abandoning Greece in its pain?
> AGAMEMNON Greece, like you, is the victim of some god.
> MENELAUS Revel in the power of your crown. Betray your brother. I shall make new plans and other friends.

DRAMATIC ACTION AND ILLUSION OF CHARACTER

The world of the play this scene is set in is one caught up in a civil war. The text was written during a civil war. To call someone a traitor within this world is provocative. The scene of dueling stories is meant to provoke the audience to question who is right. The episode: THE HOT-HEADED MAN IS FURIOUS THAT THE CHORUS DOESN'T SIDE WITH HIM. At this point in the play a Messenger arrives to announce that Iphigenia has arrived.

The text alternates between personal attack, moralizing, the story of Helen, and the personal emotions expressed while saying all this. To play the text with fourth-wall realism motivated by accomplishing tasks and encountering obstacles would prompt the cutting of long passages that seem not only un-dramatic but anti-dramatic. Analyzing the stories as stories, not just dialogue, reveals a vital way to act the scene. The speeches become dramatically active by shifting points of view. Shifting from storytelling to dialogue, the actors playing Menelaus and Agamemnon have different ways to establish character and action.

The scene can be broken apart by:

- Setting aside portions of the scene for direct address to the audience (Menelaus appeals to the Greeks for support).
- Playing the scene "realistically" (Menelaus attacks his older brother).
- Telling stories for their description of events (Menelaus demonstrates how his brother lied).
- Telling stories for their own value as episodes (MENELAUS LOSES HIS TEMPER).

The notebook pages that follow demonstrate how the stories from *Iphigenia in Aulis* can be broken down and integrated with other ways of working, including objectives and episodes. Although it isn't included in the notes, it would be possible to add work from images as well for the poised Agamemnon and the hot-headed Menelaus. From a study of the characters' words and the time the play was written, an actor could define a world of the play for *Iphigenia in Aulis* that is as equivocal as *Macbeth*'s. The highest good in this world is keeping your word. Only Iphigenia, who willingly sacrifices herself at the end of the play, seems to live up to that ideal. But is Iphigenia's sacrifice worthwhile? The playwright does not give a definite answer.

The history of the production reflects that ambivalence. Euripides died before the play could be produced, and it was staged by his nephew, who seems to have added a different ending. At the last minute, just as Agamemnon is about to plunge a knife into his daughter, Iphigenia disappears and a ram appears in her place. Of course, this doesn't happen onstage. Even Euripides's nephew had the good sense to describe such a miracle, rather than show it in a scene.

Notebook:
Applying Narrative Analysis

AGAMEMNON So, you have broken the seal and read it. It was not for your eyes.

MENELAUS Yes, I read it. I know your secrets and your shame. You will regret it.

AGAMEMNON Gods above! The arrogance of the man! Where did you waylay my messenger?

MENELAUS I was waiting for your daughter to come here from Argos.

AGAMEMNON Why?

MENELAUS Because I felt like it. I am not your slave.

AGAMEMNON This is an outrage. Am I not to be master of my own house?

MENELAUS Not when you are a cheat and a liar, when you slither your way into everything.

AGAMEMNON You talk to me of cheating and of lying. You! I hate a facile, quick tongue.

MENELAUS And I hate a devious, quick mind. You know neither justice nor honesty. I will prove your guilt. No lies, my brother! No quick denials. You cannot bluff your way out of this.

Listen to me. <u>I will not be too hard on you.</u> Do you remember your past ambitions? To be leader of the Greeks against Troy? You pretended to be reluctant. But in your heart you longed for it. And to get it you groveled. You shook everyone by the hand. Your doors were <u>open to all who wished to enter.</u> You spoke to everyone, whether they wanted to listen or not. You were nice to everyone. You wanted to be popular. You wanted no rivals.

EPISODE: MENELAUS CATCHES
HIS OLDER BROTHER DOING WRONG

Agamemnon's task:
to save his daughter
Action: *to brush off Menelaus*
Obstacle: his brother has proof

Menelaus's task:
to repossess his wife
Action: *to slap Agamemnon into action*
Obstacle: his brother's poise

Menelaus's Story:
P.O.V. Projected to the audience, personified as the Greek army.
Task: *to persuade the army*
Obstacle: their respect for their commander

Story apparatus:
<u>I will not be too hard on you.</u>
Revealing his task, *to expose his brother in public*
Event: *When Agamemnon wanted to win election, he bribed the Greeks with condescension*

Quote: <u>. . .open to all who wished to enter</u>, solicitous and oily

But then when you were made commander-in-chief, you changed your tune. You abandoned all your old friends. You were inaccessible. You locked your doors. You rarely appeared in public. Brother, a good man does not change when he gets on in the world. That is precisely the time when his friends ought to be able to count on him, when his power and success allow him to do more for them than ever. <u>This is my first point</u>, my first reproach—your lack of character.

Event: *When Agamemnon got what he wanted, he was stand-offish as usual*

Change in P.O.V.: <u>This is my first point</u> Projected to the audience, still to persuade them, by demonstrating his good will. Coldly, in order to prove he's impartial

<u>Then</u>, when the Greek army came here to Aulis and we were denied a favoring wind, you became the lowest of the low. This injunction of the gods filled you with fear. The Greeks shouted at you, demanded that the fleet turn back, that you put an end to this futile delay. One could see the distress on your face. You could not bear the thought of not launching your thousand ships, of not filling the fields of Troy with the cries of war. So you came to me. "<u>What shall I do? How can I get out of this?</u>" You were afraid of losing your command, losing the glory.

Story apparatus: <u>Then</u>
Task: *to point out the pattern of wrongdoing*

Event: *Crises came, Agamemnon was paralyzed*

Quote: "<u>What shall I do?</u> . . ."
Task?: *to beg, to rescue,*
Transaction?: *I'll humble myself / you'll help me*

<u>Then</u> Calchas spoke. You were to sacrifice your daughter. Only then would the Greeks be free to sail to Troy. You were quick to make promises. And your heart smiled. No one forced you to do what you did next. You cannot say that. You sent word to your wife that your daughter was to come to Aulis and be married to Achilles. That was the pretext you devised.

Story apparatus: <u>Then</u>
Pointing out again that this is the pattern of Agamemnon's duplicity

Event: *Agamemnon agreed to sacrifice his daughter so the ships could sail*

Event: *Agamemnon has gone back on his word*

And now? You have been caught red-handed. You have changed your mind and sent a different message. <u>You are no longer prepared to be your daughter's killer.</u>

Quote: <u>You are no longer prepared to be your daughter's killer.</u> Display the words, don't quote them.
P.O.V. held at a distance, with distaste.

I cannot be more blunt. <u>This is the same heaven that bore witness to your oaths.</u> Think! You are not unique. Many a man has worked hard to gain power. And many a man has lost that power in shame. Sometimes it is the fault of the people. They do not understand the complexity of power. But just as often it is the man himself who is incompetent and fails to protect the interests of the people. <u>My tears are for Greece.</u> She planned an action steeped in glory. Now she must suffer the mockery of barbarians. <u>All because of you and your daughter.</u> It is not courage that makes a great leader or a great general. It is intelligence. A man who has half a brain can be governor of a state. But a commander-in-chief must be blessed with intelligence.

CHORUS When brothers fight and anger and recrimination fly between them, there is only sorrow.

AGAMEMNON <u>Now it is my turn to criticize you.</u> I will be compassionate, not arrogant. I will show you the respect due a brother. Compassion springs from a good heart. Tell me first why you are so angry. You are short of breath, your face is flushed. Why? Who has done you wrong? What do you want? Do you desire to win yourself a good wife? I cannot help you there. You had no control over the one you had.

You made the mistakes. Must *I* pay for them? *I* do not have an adulteress for a wife. You talk of my ambition. But it is not *that* which torments you. No. You long to hold a beautiful woman in your arms. Discretion and common decency mean nothing to you. Your passions make you grovel. You have become an evil man. If I have the intelligence to undo a previous mistake, am I to be called a fool?

This is the same heaven that bore witness to your oaths:
Change in P.O.V.: Identifying more, less distant.

Change in P.O.V.:
<u>My tears are for Greece</u>
Task: *to egg on the listeners*
Obstacle: they don't take sides

<u>All because of you and your daughter:</u>
EPISODE: MENELAUS LOSES HIS TEMPER (Note: in the world of this play, losing your temper is weak and makes you lose status)
Task?: *to arouse the Greeks to strip Agamemnon of his command*

The Chorus's Story:
To balance the attack with the rule of respect due to the commander

Agamemnon's Story:
Story apparatus:
<u>Now it is my turn to criticize you</u>.
Task: *to establish his objectivity*
(In the world of this play, calm brings honor)

Event: *Menelaus began all this because he couldn't keep his wife at home*

Change in P.O.V.: Alternating between two tasks: *to scold his brother* and *to appeal to the audience,* personified as people in a similar crisis (when the play was first performed)

You are the fool. You lost a faithless wife and now you want her back—be the gods willing. Think back. The suitors who pursued Helen swore all manner of oaths to her father. But *you* won her hand. Not through strength or virtue but by the help of a goddess—the goddess of Hope. You want an army? Conscript the suitors! Be their general! They were fools before, why not now? But the gods are not fools. They know when an oath has been sworn under duress and when a promise is evil.

I will not kill my child. Why should you, with no concern for what is right, take vengeance on a worthless wife and live a life of happiness and success while I am forced to weep unending tears for my sins, my unjust unconscionable sins against my own child?

I shall say no more. I have been brief and to the point. If you will not see sense, that is your choice. But I must follow my conscience and do what I must do.

CHORUS Your words have changed—for the better. You now refuse to harm your child.

MENELAUS Then I am alone. I have no friends.

AGAMEMNON Not true. Simply stop destroying the friends that you have.

MENELAUS Are you our father's son!? Prove it!

AGAMEMNON We should be brothers in virtue, not in sin.

MENELAUS If you *were* my friend, you would share in my misfortunes.

AGAMEMNON Brother, you hurt me. If you chastise me, do it with some good in mind.

MENELAUS Are you abandoning Greece in its pain?

AGAMEMNON Greece, like you, is the victim of some god.

MENELAUS Revel in the power of your crown. Betray your brother. I shall make new plans and other friends.

Event: *The Greeks kept their oath* (Biased P.O.V.: And they were fools to do it)
Change in P.O.V.:
Alternating between two tasks:
to scold his brother and
to appeal to the listeners

Change in P.O.V.:
I will not kill my child. Increasingly less distanced and more identified with what he is saying
EPISODE: AGAMEMNON PUBLICLY GOES BACK ON HIS PROMISE

Story apparatus:
I have been brief, to temper the army and his brother

EPISODE:
THE CHORUS STAYS IMPARTIAL

EPISODE: THE HOT-HEADED MAN IS FURIOUS THAT THE CHORUS DOESN'T SIDE WITH HIM
Agamemnon's task:
to calm his brother
Obstacle: Menelaus's passion

Menelaus's task:
to shame his brother
Obstacle: Agamemnon won't take the bait and stays serene

Practical Tips for Working

Spare us your feelings, limit your emotional recall

During the relatively short time that realistic dramas have been performed realistically, stories told onstage have been interpreted as aspects of one character's relationship to another. According to these rules, when there is no one else onstage, actors telling a story are meant to establish an emotional relationship with themselves. The character's task is *to release the memory* of what is being described; obstacles include anything that blocks those memories, including personal inhibitions. Among actors who find a parallel with in-character storytelling and Lee Strasberg's emotional recall exercises, successful narrators overcome those blocks and arrive at the emotional state described in the story.

The search for a private image to parallel the story being told propels actors to unlock their personal histories. It doesn't always happen. Not even storytelling during psychoanalytic therapy—from which emotional recall exercises derive—can reliably reproduce an emotional state from the past. In therapy, as in performance, the process is undependable, which makes it a daring choice to try and get away with onstage.

When emotional recall works it can be thrilling, and for all the wrong reasons. It's easy for the drama of a performer accessing the past to distract the audience from the action of the play. When an actor's pathology floods the text with a wash of emotion, the audience can't help but notice the performer is elated or terrified—or working hard to get that way—but what has happened to the character or the plot of the play is drowned in oil.

From the audience's side of the stage, self-manipulation isn't dramatic, it's just selfish. Emotional recall during storytelling is very selfish, not only because it ignores the needs of the audience and the intentions of the author; it reduces the other actors to props and the lines of the play to Muzak on your solo elevator ride to catharsis.

There are legitimate ways to contain storytelling within the fourth wall: the telling of the story can itself be a task, as it is when storytelling defies authority or tries to stir other characters to action. Yet, when the task is *to defy* or *to seduce* or *to alarm* by telling a story, a performer is returned to the technical problem of how storytelling is different from enactment (and very different from emotional memory, which has no task but self-exploration).

Strasberg intended to restrict emotional recall exercises to the classroom or rehearsal hall, but, inevitably, emotional recall seeped into performance technique. Emotional recall does have its uses in film, since self-involved performances can be compensated for with interspersed reaction shots of other actors. But unlike watching a film, what the audience sees onstage cannot be selected from one successful performance among twenty failed ones. When self-indulgent emotional recall isn't confusing or boring an audience at the expense of the story, the search for personal metaphors as a stage technique exhausts the patience of the other actors and saps the progress of rehearsals.

Remember, don't relive

Emotional memory is undependable and it's selfish. It's also baloney that emotional recall is always true to life. When a criminal tells his tale, or a victim gives testimony, or a long-married couple look through their wedding album, they usually do not relive past events. They *remember* them. That's very, very different. On any given episode of *Court TV* you can witness for yourself something not unlike the following:

> DISGRUNTLED HOUSEWIFE (*coldly*) I hit him with the bottle three times. (*pause, thinking*) No. Four. Then he moved over to the bed and . . . (*pause, small smile*) No. It was a couch. Yes. Yes, it was a couch.

Or, visiting your happily married friends:

> LONG-MARRIED WIFE LEAFING THROUGH WEDDING ALBUM (*warmly*) Look, dear, there's that photograph of your Aunt Matilda. (*pause, small frown*) But wait. Who is that man with her? That's not Uncle Bob. Who is that?

The process of remembering has its own successes and failures. How many times did Disgruntled Housewife smack him? Who was Matilda dating before she met Bob? What seemed hot then (the disco-fever sideburns on Aunt Matilda's beau, the Housewife's feeling of getting even with the creep) is going to be remembered coldly now, and vice versa. The success of remembering has its own tasks and its own emotions when those tasks are accomplished—or encounter an obstacle.

> DISGRUNTLED HOUSEWIFE (*calmly*) It was *four* times I hit him. (*pause for thought, followed by smile*) No-o-o . . . It was three.

What makes you laugh now may be exactly what embarrassed you years before. What you laughed at years earlier might embarrass you now.

> LONG-MARRIED WIFE LEAFING THROUGH WEDDING ALBUM Oh, yes! (*laughing*) I remember, it's that man she hit over the head with a bottle! My, that was embarrassing! (*laughing more*) I nearly died of shame!! (*giggling*)

Have the telling of the story be an episode

Try to make the telling of the story be an episode. Have the audience notice that something has changed by the time you conclude your story. This is especially true of stories told as songs. Otherwise, the music blankets the drama and the song is a pause, not a continuation of the dramatic action.

A physical change in the storyteller—like the character of Edgar in *King Lear*, who transforms himself onstage into a beggar—will tell the audience that the story has dramatic significance as an episode. The environment can be changed in the telling of a story, too.

Learn from Mei Lanfang's sleeves

The arms of Mei Lanfang's traditional costumes ended in long-hanging sleeves. The great Chinese actor waved them like water to illustrate a description, set them in the air to flutter like a dove, let them hang over his hands, or rolled them back in character. They could be scenery, commentary, characterization—even birds. You might not have long-hanging sleeves, but anything else you might carry on with you to the stage—costume, prop, make-up—and anything you might find on the stage, scenery and lighting included, can be used to relay the event to the audience.

Imagine a retired general in a rest home fighting his old battles again—over lunch. He uses his salt and pepper shakers as enemy cannons, the folded napkin as a sand dune. The fork and the knife are two wings of the army—until the water glass gets in the way. The general's lunch table has a meaning of its own: it's the battlefield. The water glass can spill and the napkin can unfold in order to represent the blowing away of the sand dune.

In the general's storytelling, if the napkin is the last brave soldier, when the general puts the napkin back in his pocket, the soldier dies, or retreats. When the general crushes the napkin, he crushes the soldier. In all of these actions the general has the possibility of rendering the passage of time through his pace and rhythm.

It is important to think that as an actor telling the story, you have the same relationship to the props and costumes as a puppeteer to a puppet show. Onstage, you can use a table, a chair, a salt-shaker, or your handkerchief—even the sleeve of your costume—to tell the story.

Simplify character quotes

A word of caution. Too much impersonation during a character quote defeats the purpose of the story. It's supposed to be different from enactment; it need not be a detailed impression. Simpler character quotes invite the audience to participate in fleshing out the character.

Take advantage of the stage's freedom by thinking of a film's freedom

As storyteller, you have control over the audience's perception. You can send them flying over the seas or burrowing into the head of the villain. Use this power to present events the way a film editor combines camera angles to create a sophisticated, multidimensional approach when depicting a scene.

Novels also make a good model. Eighteenth-century writers structured their novels as collections of letters from different people describing the same events. If you like a challenge, you could look to a novel written in the twentieth century: *Hopscotch* by the Argentine writer Julio Cortázar, first published in Spanish in 1963. *Hopscotch* turns a shift of view into the playful game of the title.* The first fifty-six short chapters can be read in order and the book be done with. Or, as Cortázar suggests in a "Table of Instructions," the reader may begin with Chapter 73, jump back to Chapters 1 and 2, leap forward to chapter 166, back to Chapter 3, and skip over to 84, in a pattern that concludes with Chapter 131—hopping backward from Chapter 155 between 64 and 123. . . . Of course, you could read the chapters in the order that they're printed or in an order of your own.

It is with the art form of the twentieth century—the cinema—that the alternation of points of view achieved greatness as a narrative technique, complete with a history and vocabulary of its own. From the beginnings of the epic cinema—D.W. Griffith's *Intolerance* and Abel Gance's *Napoleon*—the permutations of shifting points of view have revealed a new way to conceive of human relationships, including character and the meaning of behavior.† Relativity is not just a theory of Einstein; it is the worldview of our time as surely as motivation was the worldview of Stanislavsky and Freud.

Learn from Mae West . . . to pause

While telling a story, you control time—for the events and for the audience. Your listeners can hang on your every word or be left behind. Mae West's trick was to pause in order to give her audience time to receive the performance and think about what they'd just been told. It's a good way to make sure listeners understand and have time to react. The audience is your partner in the creation of the illusions of character and dramatic action, and they need time to do their work. Give them that time.

Don't speed up for a long story out of a fear that the audience will lose interest over time. It works the other way around. You'll lose them if you go too fast, because they won't have time to take in the significance of events, character quotes, and descriptions. Take your time, make your points. Just as the passion you have for an image transfers to the audience, so too will your interest in a story get the audience interested as well.

There are exceptions

Some stories are told without dramatic action or character or events. Recitations, for instance, have no character and often no dramatic action. Some reports keep a distanced point of view that does not change. Therefore, the report itself is not a dramatic action but part of a larger action. Unvarying emotional display has the same effect: static by itself, but useful in a larger design.

Not every story is important for the information value of its words. Sometimes a story is meant to be like birdsong; the sound of a speaker is intended to sooth, to seduce, to baffle. Sometimes the action of simply *speaking* is significant, as in Beckett or Ionesco.

Rayuela in Spanish.

†Griffith derived the use of close-ups alternating with longer shots of the same scene from techniques used by Dickens in his novels.

When asked, interrupt realistic behavior with storytelling

Sometimes a director or an adventurous playwright will ask a performer to juxtapose storytelling techniques within detailed realistic scenes. This use of mixed techniques resembles a Cubist painting with a composition impossible to view in life: the bottom of a bottle, the hole in a guitar, the profile of a wineglass—all these curves in contrast to the checkered pattern of a tablecloth as seen from above. Working like this onstage, an actor separates narrative lines from dialogue and tells the story of the scene directly to the audience. When the behavior of a role is held up for such a discussion, the contrast between the character's thoughts and actions are set out as sharply as the wineglass against the checkered tablecloth.

In some Cubist paintings there are real objects—scraps of newspaper, wallpaper, a train ticket—pasted onto the canvas next to a splat of paint. The Spanish Cubist Juan Gris could fake wood grain so well that he fooled the eye—next to his convincing "wood" he'd paint an obviously splotchy spread of polka dots. Such a dynamic and exciting juxtaposition of techniques can be used in acting to similar effect, when a narrative approach to dramatic text is combined within a "realistic" scene.

It is difficult to volunteer storytelling techniques unless the director agrees. Certain directors encourage actors to mix narration with enactment: in America, Richard Schechner and Anne Bogart (among others); in Western Europe, Ariane Mnouckine and Peter Brook; in Eastern Europe, Lev Dodin and Jerzy Grotowski; in Japan, Suzuki. For some directors—and litigious playwrights—it is disrespectful to the text and the author's intentions.

Onstage narration is neither off-putting nor strange in the middle of a scene. The best known example (so well known as to be unnoticed) is the use of an *aside*. An aside's switch from the dramatic to narrative establishes a personal relationship of confidence with the audience. In no way does an aside diminish the illusion of a character being created; on the contrary, it reinforces the characterization. If the style or the aesthetics of the production permit the liberty, storytelling techniques woven into the texture of a realistic scene enhance characterization and dramatic action.

Storytelling Within Enactment: Rehearsing a Scene from *The Three Sisters*

Let's look at the last scene from Chekhov's 1904 play *The Three Sisters* (106)—a text with a history of being performed rather than narrated—for the possibilities of storytelling. As a creative artist, as well as an interpretive one, an actor can choose to include storytelling even in texts that seem to require enactment exclusively. Proust, speaking about "realism," says the real problem with "realism" is that, over time, it teaches us to mistake its formulae for reality.

Irina (pronounced e-REE-na) and Olga are two of the three sisters who live in a provincial town. Anfisa (An-FEE-za) is their old nurse, whom they still call by the childish name of Nana. Vershinin (Ver-SHEEN-in) is an army officer in love with the third sister, Masha (who is not in this scene). The play, in part, is about the way hope withers with time. The sisters have hoped to escape provincial life and go to Moscow. Vershinin and Masha have hoped for a true love together, outside of their marriages to other people.

This is the day Vershinin's division of soldiers, the central point of the sisters' lives, is leaving town. The scene occurs in the last act of the play, in the garden of the sisters' family house, now taken over by their sister-in-law. The first three acts have taken place indoors; now the sisters are sitting outside in the garden, which is intruded on by outsiders. The shift in the scene from indoors to outdoors would support a change in point of view for the speakers, turned out of their home, crowded in the garden, with nowhere to turn but the audience. Throughout the play, characters crowd in on each other. Deeply felt confidences are poured out to whomever happens to be in the room. Here, out in the garden, that pressure might force those confidences toward the listening audience.

> *Two street musicians, a man and a girl, play on the violin and harp;* VERSHININ, OLGA, *and* ANFISA *come out of the house and listen in silence for a moment;* IRINA *approaches.*

> IRINA Our garden's like a public thoroughfare; people keep walking and driving through it. Nurse, give those musicians something.

Why can't Irina split the focus of her lines and announce to the audience, not her nurse, that the garden is overrun? Because this is not the style that Stanislavsky used when he directed the play? Chekhov himself objected to the realistic style of Stanislavsky's direction in letters to Meyerhold, who played the important role of Tuzenbach for Stanislavsky in the original production.

> ANFISA (*gives money to the musicians*) Go along and God bless you, good people. (*the musicians bow and leave*) Poor things! You don't go around playing like that if you're well-fed.

The old nurse Anfisa will, at first, retain the focus of the scene onstage when she speaks to the onstage musicians, although her comment about them might be made to the audience. Another choice might be that Anfisa is unaware of the audience until they laugh at her comment. Notice that, in the scene that follows, she calls the sisters by their childhood names: Arisha, Olyusha, and Mashenka.

> ANFISA (*to* IRINA) Good day, Arisha! (*kisses her*) Ee-e, little one, what a life I am having! What a life! What a life!

It is possible to justify the repetition of the words "What a life!"—often obscured in translation by one emphatic sentence, rather than two—by performing them in two different ways: the first as a declaration to Irina, the second as a report to the audience.

TELLING A STORY

There's even a characteristic task to be found: Old Anfisa would enjoy a chance to boast to and tell her story to a crowd.

> ANFISA What a life! What a life! Living at the high school in a government apartment with Olyusha—that's what God has granted me in my old age. Never in my life have I lived like this, sinner that I am . . . A big government apartment, a whole room to myself, my own bed. All at government expense. I wake up in the night and—oh, Lord, Mother of God, there's not a happier person in the world!

Storytelling doesn't take away from the reality of Anfisa as a character; it increases the illusion of character by allowing her to tell her listeners about her new life. The next part of the scene might be left as observed behavior. Vershinin is speaking of the army division:

> VERSHININ (*looking at his watch*) We shall be leaving directly, Olga Serge-yevna. Time to be off. (*pause*) I wish you everything, everything . . . Where is Maria Sergeyevna?
>
> IRINA She's somewhere in the garden . . . I'll go and look for her.
>
> VERSHININ Please be so kind. I must hurry.
>
> ANFISA I'll go look for her, too. (*calls*) Mashenka, aa-oo! (*goes with* IRINA *to the rear of the garden*) Aa-oo, aa-oo!
>
> VERSHININ All things come to an end.

If Vershinin speaks "all things come to an end" to the audience, the switch from enactment to storytelling will create its own dramatic action. It will be as if the soul of the character is speaking, having left the body of the role. Vershinin tells the audience that his hopes are gone; that there will be no love affair with Masha—not even a satisfying goodbye. He's announcing other dreams in the play are coming to an end as well.

Speaking these lines to the audience can also make it appear that the actor has stepped *out* of the role, alienating—in Brecht's terms—the meaning of the lines so that they comment on the action of the play itself, which is now coming to an end. If such a decision is made to alienate the lines—the actor and not "Vershinin" speaking them—the dramatic effect will be striking and harsh. The words are the announcements of the episode, now told as an event: ALL THINGS COME TO AN END.

Said to the audience from the point of view of the role, however, the words offer up Vershinin's response to a number of finales: the end of his affair with Masha, the end of the army in the three sisters' life, and the end of the play itself. The other actors on-stage don't have to pretend they don't notice that Vershinin is speaking to the audience. They can react—in character, or not—as if the thought that their dreams have ended had passed through all their minds and stirred up various responses. The words "all things come to an end" will now hover over the "realistic" scene that follows.

The return to enactment after narration can be very moving. This way, the audience has had a chance to appreciate, judge, and sympathize with the *web of relationships*. The characters act heroically, because they are pressing on despite knowledge of their inevitable failure. Openly including the character's—or the actor's—understanding of the end of the role as part of the performance will create an understanding of the characters among the audience that exceeds observation.

> VERSHININ Here we are parting. (*looks at his watch*) The town gave us a sort of lunch, we had champagne, the Mayor made a speech, I ate and listened, but in my heart I was here with you . . . (*looks around the garden*) I've grown attached to you.

Olga could emphasize the event by asking her question to the listening audience.

> OLGA Shall we meet again some day?
> VERSHININ Probably not. (*pause*)

Vershinin's comment would be funny as story apparatus told to the audience.

> VERSHININ My wife and the two little girls will remain here for another month or two; please, if anything happens, or if they need anything . . .
> OLGA Yes, yes, of course. You needn't worry. (*pause*) By tomorrow there won't be a single officer or soldier in town; it will all be a memory, and for us, of course, a new life will begin . . . (*pause*)

Olga's faith can be established by the way she tells this story to the audience, and established just as strongly, if not more so, than if she said the same words to Vershinin. It won't deny emotion to the scene by ripping the web of relationships between characters that is claimed to be the basis for the audience's interest. Narration engages the audience in a different way, by letting them play the scene in their minds.

> OLGA Nothing ever happens the way we want it to. I didn't want to be a headmistress, and yet I became one. It means we are not to be in Moscow . . .

In telling this story, does Olga identify with the *I* in her story? Maybe. Or is she emotionally distanced, speaking as if the *I* was a third person? Does she laugh? Maybe. To whom is Olga saying "Nothing ever happens the way we want it to"? Why not address it to a projected audience? How is such an audience characterized? Should the audience be characterized as modern-day Russians, who might cry at such a sentiment?

There are many examples of familiar texts written to combine narration with performance that are now performed without narration, because the "realistic" style of the twentieth century has obscured the memory of other approaches. The most significant are the stories written by Shakespeare, called *soliloquies*, the subject of the next chapter.

CHAPTER 3

SHAKESPEARE'S SOLILOQUIES

A **soliloquy** is a speech said by an actor onstage and alone. This is not the same thing as being onstage and alone and speaking to yourself. By being loud enough to be overheard, even in a soliloquy, performers acknowledge the presence of a listening audience and their obligation to communicate—not just express themselves like introspective songbirds spied on in the woods.

In a soliloquy, the story of a role's inner thoughts and feelings is told with a characterization projected onto the audience; a characterization that reflects the speaker. In short, you address the audience as if they were an aspect of yourself. This is what distinguishes soliloquies from Shakespeare's prologues, epilogues, and choruses, in which actors frankly address the audience as audience.

An actor performing a soliloquy is still meant to report to the audience, not muse. As the Greek God Comus is supposed to have pointed out—and the British novelist Laurence Sterne repeated—people aren't made of glass. If an artist invites an audience to enjoy the inner drama of a role, there must be some way to expose that inner drama to common sight. Actors performing Shakespeare's soliloquies speak directly to describe and demonstrate what's going on beneath the surface of the role.

Playing a soliloquy without acknowledging the audience is one of many conventions well-meaning actors have applied to speaking Shakespeare's words during four centuries of performance history. Sliding an invisible fourth wall between a speaker and listeners is not just an interpretation; it is something more intrusive. Over time, such additions to an artwork obscure that they are additions and become mistaken for the artwork itself. This is true not only for plays, but for other forms of art to which meanings have been added over time. A good example is the story of a once famous classical Greek sculpture called *Zingara*—Italian for "gypsy woman," which is what the statue depicts.

Zingara was highly praised during the seventeenth century and still quite popular in the eighteenth and mid-nineteenth centuries. Connoisseurs wrote at length about the cunning gypsy expression "on the lookout for dupes" (107). The work was especially valued among scholars as evidence of gypsies during the classic period of the Greeks and Romans. Edmund Gibbon, the celebrated author of *The Decline and Fall of the Roman Empire* (1776–1788) wrote of the statue's "true character of impudence and low cunning suitable to a fortune-teller" (108).

The *Zingara* had been in the collection of the Italian Borghese family for at least a century and a half when, in 1807, Prince Camillo Borghese sold it to his brother-in-law,

Napoleon Bonaparte. Napoleon added this prize to the collection at the Louvre, where it was affectionately known as "La Petite Bohémienne." At first. Today, the *Zingara* is deposited at Versailles and languishes in obscurity—its "gypsy" character is more fraud than any fortune-teller's.

The marble section of the work is, without a doubt, fourth-century Greek, but it depicts nothing more than folded drapery. The bronze "gypsy" head, hands, and feet were stuck on to the ends of the marble over fifteen-hundred years after it was first carved—by a French sculptor working on Borghese orders. If you need an image for *cunning*, don't think of the statue; think of the expression on the Prince's face after he sold the thing to Napoleon.

When you treat an Elizabethan soliloquy as a chance for spied-on soul-searching, you are doing the same thing as adding the gypsy's head, changing and obscuring the meaning of the original. Even though the convention of talking to yourself may have been accepted for a hundred and fifty years, like the smiling Italian prince, you are selling a false bill of goods.

If you reread the soliloquies written by Shakespeare with an eye to their storytelling opportunities, you will see storytelling well supported by the text. Like other stories told onstage, performing a soliloquy to an audience can be an episode by itself. The way a soliloquy is told onstage will characterize the speaker's role, and a shift in the point of view of the narrator will create dramatic action. Shakespeare's particular use of storytelling has further opportunities for characterization and action, as we'll see.

Share Your Thoughts with the Audience: Rehearsing *Romeo and Juliet*

Let's start with a speech made overly familiar by its excellence:

ROMEO But, soft! what light through yonder window breaks?

Romeo and Juliet, Act II, scene ii

To whom is Romeo talking? We all know—having seen the speech parodied endless times, even by the Flintstones—that Romeo is supposed to be deep in contemplation, talking to himself. But the words the character speaks are not contemplative; they are an over-eager, one-sided conversation. The listening audience is characterized as a friend with whom the would-be lover shares his confidence, or, in Romeo's case, lack of confidence.

When this scene was first staged, the role of Juliet was played by a boy. There was no scenery, there were no lighting effects. It was daytime at the Globe Theater. In order to set the scene, the actor playing Romeo first had to tell the audience who was who and what was what. So the soliloquy began with an announcement of the event: *That's supposed to be the girl I love, and it's supposed to be night, and she's supposed to be radiantly beautiful in the moonlight.*

TELLING A STORY

Shakespeare put it much better:

ROMEO It is the east, and Juliet is the sun!

Now that that's been made clear, Romeo can speak to Juliet, although at a distance, please, and from a *distanced point of view*, according to the poetic conventions of the time.

ROMEO Arise, fair sun, and kill the envious moon,
    Who is already sick and pale with grief,
    That thou her maid art far more fair than she:
    Be not her maid, since she is envious;
    Her vestal livery is but sick and green,
    And none but fools do wear it; cast it off.

The point of views *shifts* as Romeo identifies with what he describes:

ROMEO It is my lady; O, it is my love!
    O, that she knew she were!

The unsure way the story is told characterizes Romeo with an adolescent blend of boldness and uncertainty. The events are described—

ROMEO She speaks, yet she says nothing.

—but the storyteller is unsure what the events signify. Is it an invitation for him to approach?

ROMEO What of that?
    Her eye discourses, I will answer it.

As he lurches forward—and balks—Romeo makes an excuse to the audience for his shyness:

ROMEO I am too bold; 'tis not to me she speaks.

If he cannot talk to her, he can at least talk *about* her. The description that follows sets a scene in the theater of the audience's mind. The actor and the character—and the playwright—enjoy their fantasies more by sharing them.

ROMEO Two of the fairest stars in all the heaven,
    Having some business do entreat her eyes
    To twinkle in their spheres till they return.

Like someone telling a riddle, Romeo sets up a question for his listeners.

ROMEO What if her eyes were there, they in her head?

He can answer his own question, and brag some more about the girl he would like to have as his lover.

ROMEO The brightness of her cheek would shame those stars,
    As daylight doth a lamp; her eyes in heaven
    Would through the airy region stream so bright
    That birds would sing, and think it were not night.

It's a lot more fun to brag to other people than to yourself. Speaking this lush poetry to himself would characterize Romeo as self-absorbed, in love with his own ability to make metaphors. The character is interpreted as such whenever he's shoved behind the fourth wall. But as a story told to an audience, the point of view demonstrates the narrator's exuberance and characterizes both roles at once.

Although the boy playing Juliet enacted the scene by moving his hand, it was the actor playing Romeo who told the audience what that movement meant and how much it moved him to watch it.

ROMEO See how she leans her cheek upon her hand!

Romeo is now intimate enough with the listening audience to reveal his desire.

ROMEO O, that I were a glove upon that hand,
    That I might touch that cheek!

Saying the words of this soliloquy, any actor playing Romeo is meant to generously share the hopes, dreams, and fears of the character. Even his famous opening lines— "But, soft!"—don't have to be said to himself. They can be directed to the audience as a command: *Shhh! Be quiet. Don't scare away the girl in the window.*

When Romeo's doubts and hopes and desires are reported directly to the audience, the soliloquy is active and vigorous, not pensive or meandering. Don't talk to yourself unless you have to. It's a lot easier, and a lot more interesting, if you talk to someone else. Yes, of course, talk to Juliet in her balcony. But talk to the matinee ladies in *their* balcony, too. Unlike Juliet, the ladies in the balcony will announce the episode for you. "Oh, look," they will say to each other (and anyone else within earshot). "He wants to be with her and he's afraid to act on it. So young!"

Telling the Audience What They Already Know: Bottom from *A Midsummer Night's Dream*

One special feature of Shakespeare's soliloquies is that sometimes a character describes a scene after it takes place. When an audience has already seen what the character describes, they can better assess the storyteller's point of view—and collaborate to characterize the role of the speaker.

After Richard III pledges his love to Lady Anne, as soon as Anne leaves and Richard is alone onstage, the actor playing the role gets to crow out his version of what just happened and show himself off as an eager hypocrite and shameless liar.

> RICHARD Was ever woman in this humor wooed? . . .
> I'll have her; but I will not keep her long.
> What! I, that kill'd her husband and his father,
> To take her in her heart's extremest hate;
> With curses in her mouth, tears in her eyes,
> The bleeding witness of my hatred by;
> Having God, her conscience, and these bars against me,
> And I no friends to back my suit withal,
> But the plain devil and dissembling looks,
> And yet to win her, all the world to nothing!
> Ha!

> *Richard III, Act I, scene ii*

The audience has just witnessed for itself the hypocritical love scene Richard describes. After he tells the story, the cunning and cruelty of his role is reinforced.

An actor describing a scene after the fact can reveal a role's motives as well as character, but description can also reveal that the character is lost to the meaning of what he describes. In *A Midsummer Night's Dream*, the Queen of the Fairies is bound by a spell to make love to a man so low his name is Bottom—a dolt with the magically added ugliness of an ass's head. The audience is shown their grotesque courtship and lovemaking, as well as the scene when the Fairy Queen abandons the sleeping Bottom in disgust and returns to her fairy kingdom. Alone onstage, Bottom ends his sleep with a start, thinking he is where he was when last awake: at a rehearsal for a play.

> BOTTOM (*waking*) When my cue comes, call me, and I will answer . . .

> *A Midsummer Night's Dream, Act IV, scene i*

Shakespeare has characters wake with a start and blurt words to the air in other plays as well, the better to distinguish that the rest of the lines are spoken directly to the audience and not to the air. Once Bottom understands he is alone, he stops looking around the stage for the other actors and tells the audience what it already knows:

> BOTTOM I have had a most rare vision.

The audience has seen this vision. The question is, what will Bottom say about it? What will he remember? How will he describe it?

BOTTOM I have had a dream, past the wit of man to say what dream it was.

Not very articulate, is he?

BOTTOM Man is but an ass if he go about to expound this dream. Methought I was—there is no man can tell what. Methought I was, and methought I had—but man is but a patch'd fool, if he will offer to say what methought I had.

The joke, of course, is that he was an ass. He knows it, the audience knows it, the audience knows he knows it, and now the audience knows more: that Bottom is too proud to admit he was an ass. You may interpret his hesitations to mean that his erotic adventure is too embarrassing—or stimulating—for him to talk about. Either way, how he tells the story is weighed by the audience's knowledge—not the character's ignorance—to characterize Bottom as ass or prude or lecher.

Bottom's inability to describe or appreciate what he has experienced reveals the limits of his understanding and expression, and in turn tells the audience who Bottom is. The description that follows tells the audience still more: Bottom is a *blowhard*.

BOTTOM The eye of man hath not heard, the ear of man hath not seen, man's hand is not able to taste, his tongue to conceive, nor his heart to report what my dream was.

Not just a blowhard, he's a show-off, too:

BOTTOM I will get Peter Quince to write a ballad of this dream. It shall be call'd Bottom's Dream, because it hath no bottom; and I will sing it in the latter end of a play, before the Duke . . .

The character of Bottom is reinforced by the way he tells his story, especially because the audience knows from the play that his visit to the fairy kingdom offers sumptuous possibilities for description.

Establish Dramatic Action by What Happens to You as You Tell the Story: Don Armado from *Love's Labour's Lost*

Speaking a soliloquy is itself a dramatic action and can often be an episode with a beginning, middle, and end. Romeo talks himself out of saying hello; Bottom talks himself from ass to playwright. For five acts (and four and a half hours), Hamlet talks himself in and out of revenge. In various comedies, Shakespeare gives various characters soliloquies to talk themselves in and out of love. Here is a Spanish knight from *Love's Labour's Lost* doing just that:

DON ARMADO I do affect the very ground, which is base, where her shoe, which is baser, guided by her foot, which is basest, doth tread.

Love's Labour's Lost, Act I, scene ii

In order for the speech to be an episode, or to have a dramatic action, something has to change. Here, the change is the speaker's attitude to love. If an actor starts this silly soliloquy with a swooning "I do affect the very ground," the episode has begun at its conclusion and the role has no room for action.

In order to create an onstage episode, Don Armado must first try to talk himself out of love. His description of the girl is biased against her. He would like to disgust himself—and the audience—with the baseness of the girl. When that doesn't work, he switches to more logical objections. He has made an oath not to fall in love:

DON ARMADO I shall be forsworn—which is a great argument of false-hood— if I love . . .

Logic is not strong enough, either, to defend Don Armado from his feelings. His resolve wavers and his point of view *shifts* as he asks the audience to consider other great heroes who have fallen in love; heroes as strong and as wise as even Don Armado himself.

DON ARMADO Yet Samson was so tempted—and he had an excellent strength; yet was Solomon so seduced—and he had a very good wit . . .

The drama here is the change in Armado's feelings and his intentions as they weaken in opposition to what he describes. At last the Spanish knight admits "Cupid's butt-shaft is too . . . much odds for a Spaniard's rapier." Despite his supposed bravery in battle, Don Armado submits to Cupid:

DON ARMADO . . . his disgrace is to be called boy; but his glory is to subdue men.

In the course of the soliloquy, Don Armado changes his mind and announces the episode himself, although with a little fanfare first:

DON ARMADO Adieu, valour! rust, rapier! be still, drum! for your manager is in love . . .

Next is the *gest*, the act of the soldier saying the words:

DON ARMADO Yea, he loveth.

The point of view has moved from disgust to submission. Like Romeo and Bottom, Don Armado knows it's more fun to tell people about such an experience rather than keep it to yourself. He finishes with a promise to write poetry. Here, you can go right ahead and talk to the air. Talk to yourself, too. It's meant to be ridiculous.

> DON ARMADO Assist me, some extemporal god of rhyme, for I am sure I shall turn sonneteer. Devise, wit; write, pen; for I am for whole volumes in folio.

By the way, on the rare occasions when a character does speak to the air, Shakespeare often includes the word *fool*. Cressida, a Trojan princess almost as silly as Don Armado, reproaches herself for speaking her thoughts out loud in the middle of a love scene with Troilus: "See fools, why have we blabbed?" Why blab? The better to play an episode.

The Episode Involves a Change in the Relationship to the Audience: *Richard III*

When a soliloquy implies a partner, an episode will evolve onstage between the actor and the projected partner. Some soliloquies have interaction with the audience as complex as in a scene. At the beginning of *Richard III*, the villainous title character enjoys the presence of the audience, and projects onto them the character of fellow rogue. Throughout the play Richard projects the crowd's approval when they laugh at his jokes—even about murdering a child. "So young and wise, they say, do never live long," he says about the boy princes he plans to have killed.

At the end of the play Richard discovers that the audience has turned on him. Like Bottom, he wakes from a dream and speaks to himself:

> RICHARD Give me another horse—Bind up my wounds—
> Have mercy, Jesu! Soft!—

> *Richard III, Act V, scene iii*

The beginning, "Have mercy, Jesu," is said to the air. Enjoy it! Richard has been dreaming of a battle:

> RICHARD —I did but dream.
> O coward conscience, how dost thou afflict me!

Yes, he could be speaking to himself, but read a little further. It makes more sense that he is speaking to the audience, personified as *his conscience*.

> RICHARD The lights burn blue. It is now dead midnight.
> Cold fearful drops stand on my trembling flesh.

For whose benefit does Richard describe this? To reassure himself that he is in bed?

That the lamp is blue? That it's late? Doesn't it make more sense that he says these things, like the actor playing Romeo, so that the audience may picture them?

>   RICHARD What do I fear? Myself? There's none else by.

If the lines are said to the audience, personified as his accusing conscience, then the actor playing Richard may play the role of defender.

>   RICHARD Richard loves Richard; that is, I am I.
>   Is there a murderer here? No—yes, I am.

No—yes, I am? Do you want to say this to yourself by flinging your head from side to side? Wouldn't you rather say this to members of the audience on whom you *project* the role of your attackers?

>   RICHARD Then fly. What, from myself? Great reason why—
>   Lest I revenge. What, myself upon myself!

Now you can confess to the audience:

>   RICHARD Alack, I love myself. Wherefore? For any good
>   That I myself have done unto myself?
>   O, no! Alas, I rather hate myself
>   For hateful deeds committed by myself!
>   I am a villain—

Now you can defy the attacking audience:

>   RICHARD —yet I lie, I am not.

If you feel you must, speak to yourself here. The word *fool* would indicate you could.

>   RICHARD Fool, of thyself speak well. Fool, do not flatter.

Nevertheless, Shakespeare's words return you to a vision of the audience stretched out in front of you:

>   RICHARD My conscience hath a thousand several tongues,
>   And every tongue brings in a several tale,
>   And every tale condemns me for a villain.

It is much more dramatic to see your condemning judges sitting in rows than to talk to yourself. Quote them:

> RICHARD Perjury, perjury, in the high'st degree;
>   Murder, stern murder, in the dir'st degree;
>   All several sins, all us'd in each degree,
>   Throng to the bar, crying all "Guilty! guilty!"

The point of view switches here. What it changes to is a matter of interpretation. The audience seems to listen with pitiless indifference.

> RICHARD I shall despair. There is no creature loves me;
>   And if I die no soul will pity me:
>   And wherefore should they, since that I myself
>   Find in myself no pity to myself?

If you choose a distanced point of view, Richard will be describing himself coolly and dispassionately. The effect will be chilling, and the episode will become RICHARD FACES UP TO DAMNATION. If you choose to identify the speaker with the emotion he describes—despair—then the effect will be pathetic as Richard tries to pry pity from his listeners. The episode will become VILLAIN BEGS FOR PITY.

Next comes a description, very bare, of what the audience has already witnessed in the scene before.

> RICHARD Methought the souls of all that I had murder'd
>   Came to my tent, and every one did threat
>   To-morrow's vengeance on the head of Richard.

This simple statement of fact implies a more distanced point of view, and a change toward the audience, as if Richard had appeased his conscience by admitting his loss of faith. He is calm now, able to tell a story and continue the rest of the play—without fear.

Here is the line of roles projected onto the listening audience, and to which Richard responds with roles of his own.

- Consoler/Frightened Dreamer: *I did but dream*
- Intimidator/Defiant Hero: *O coward conscience, how dost thou afflict me!*
- Attacker/Defender: *Is there a murderer here? No—yes, I am*
- Confessor/Sinner: *Alack, I love myself. Wherefore? I am a villain*
- Judge/Accused: *Several sins . . . Throng to the bar, crying all "Guilty! Guilty!"*
- Indifferent Friend/Despairing Friend: *There is no creature loves me*

Grant Richard some courage and call the episode RICHARD FACES UP TO DAMNATION. The transactions will follow a pattern of trading an admission of weakness for calm. The *gest* will be spoken at first—"I myself find in myself no pity to myself"—until, in rehearsal, the actor can devise some behavior to establish the transaction. When Olivier played the role, he faced his enemies like a snarling animal and practically spat. If you remember, one of his images was the Big Bad Wolf.

Continue a Relationship with the Audience: *Macbeth*

The character of the speaker will be reflected in the characterization of the audience. Bottom speaks to an audience as dumb as he is, Richard to an audience as pitiless as himself, Don Armado to fellow knights. Different characters within the same play will personify the audience differently. Edmund in *King Lear* speaks to fellow rogues, his brother Edgar in the same play speaks to compassionate friends.

There is a continuing relationship each time the character addresses the audience. It is as if the audience was a consistent character, like any partner in a play. This happens most with Shakespeare's villains—Richard III, Edmund from *King Lear*, Iago from *Othello*. They all begin speaking with great familiar ease to their audiences, a convention borrowed from medieval morality plays in which the Devil likewise boasted of his powers. Unlike the morality plays, where the dynamic was one-sided, as in a sermon, the exchange between villain and listener in a play by Shakespeare develops as a progression, almost a subplot all its own.

Look at the relationship between Macbeth and his audience. Through all five acts, the audience is the murderer's one true friend to whom he can be honest, even in defeat. At first Macbeth makes furtive contact, done on the sly in the middle of a scene with onstage friends:

> MACBETH My thought, whose murder yet is but fantastical,
>   Shakes so my single state of man, that function
>   Is smother'd in surmise, and nothing is
>   But what is not.
> BANQUO Look, how our partner's rapt.
> MACBETH (*aside*) If chance will have me King, why, chance may crown me
>   Without my stir.
>
> *Macbeth, Act I, scene iii*

When the time comes to murder, he hopes to persuade the audience to approve:

> MACBETH If it were done when 'tis done, then 'twere well
>   It were done quickly . . .
>
> *Macbeth, Act I, scene vii*

On his way to commit the murder, Macbeth famously sees and speaks to an imaginary dagger hovering before him. Yet, even as he speaks to the air, Macbeth describes his hallucination to the audience:

> MACBETH Mine eyes are made the fools o' the other senses,
>   Or else worth all the rest. I see thee still;

And on thy blade and dudgeon gouts of blood,
Which was not so before. There's no such thing:
It is the bloody business which informs
Thus to mine eyes . . .

Macbeth, Act II, scene i

When the same speech resumes, Macbeth shares a vision with his listeners:

MACBETH Now o'er the one half-world
    Nature seems dead, and wicked dreams abuse
    The curtain'd sleep; witchcraft celebrates
    Pale Hecate's offerings; and wither'd murder,
    Alarum'd by his sentinel, the wolf,
    Whose howl's his watch, thus with his stealthy pace,
    With Tarquin's ravishing strides, towards his design
    Moves like a ghost.

The point of view expands from the personal to the universal, exactly the opposite direction a point of view usually moves—from distanced narration to emotional identification—when stories are told in a "realistic" play.

By Act III, Macbeth is King, and the audience is still the confidante to whom he may admit the truth of his new status, and his dislike of his other old friends:

MACBETH To be thus is nothing;
    But to be safely thus—our fears in Banquo
    Stick deep; and in his royalty of nature
    Reigns that which would be fear'd.

Macbeth, Act III, scene i

The character of Macbeth is that of an introspective man who wishes his nature to change to unthinking action. The transformations in his character are told to us as much as shown to us:

MACBETH . . . from this moment
    The very firstlings of my heart shall be
    The firstlings of my hand. And even now,
    To crown my thoughts with acts, be it thought and done:
    The castle of Macduff I will surprise;
    Seize upon Fife; give to the edge o' the sword
    His wife, his babes, and all unfortunate souls
    That trace him in his line.

Macbeth, Act IV, scene i

As Macbeth describes the scene to follow, the boy playing Lady Macduff, like Juliet with Romeo, would have simultaneously taken his place onstage with Macbeth's description. One of the reasons the brief scene with Lady Macduff is often cut is that it takes more time to bring the "castle of Macduff" on and off stage than it does to play the scene. It's unnecessary, though, to have a castle onstage; the actor's description of his intentions will suffice.

By the play's end the role is characterized by the heroic and unsparing way Macbeth faces up to the consequences of his crimes:

> MACBETH I have liv'd long enough: my way of life
>   Is fall'n into the sear, the yellow leaf;
>   And that which should accompany old age,
>   As honor, love, obedience, troops of friends,
>   I must not look to have; but, in their stead,
>   Curses not loud but deep, mouth-honor, breath,
>   Which the poor heart would fain deny and dare not.
>
> *Macbeth, Act V, scene iii*

From furtive aside to brutal honesty, Macbeth's continuing intimacy with the audience allows an actor to reveal aspects of the role that are otherwise difficult if not impossible to express.

Combine Techniques

In plays written by Shakespeare, Brecht, Chekhov, or Euripides, narrative analysis can be used in conjunction with the other forms of analysis described in previous chapters. The telling of a story may itself be an episode, character quotes may include Stanislavsky's tasks, and descriptive passages will depend on images. World of the play analysis helps organize the meaning of it all. Yet, even if a narrative analysis includes other methods, storytelling has a distinctive feel of its own because it relies on the audience to play the scene in their heads and so combine the different techniques of representation.

To return to the metaphor of Cubism, a Cubist painter juxtaposes a realistic drawing of the side of a glass with the abstraction of an emblem, such as the hole in the guitar, placed next to the patterns of faked (though convincing) wood grain and pasted-on wallpaper. Out of combined techniques and skills, a new beauty is formed.

Translate those painting techniques by your Rosetta Stone of acting techniques: the realistic drawing is the equivalent of a likeness constructed by tasks and actions, the hole of the guitar is an image, the wallpaper fragment evidence of the world of the play. Placed together, they create a satisfying composition like an actor's episode, and within the frame they combine to tell the story of the table top. If a painter can do all that with what the French call *nature morte*—not just still life, but *dead* life—think of what you can do to bring life to a story onstage.

www.ingramcontent.com/pod-product-compliance
Lightning Source LLC
LaVergne TN
LVHW081321060426
835509LV00015B/1619